TAKE COMMAND

FIND YOUR INNER STRENGTH,
BUILD ENDURING RELATIONSHIPS,
AND LIVE THE LIFE YOU WANT

JOE HART AND MICHAEL CROM

SIMON & SCHUSTER PAPERBACKS

NEW YORK LONDON TORONTO SYDNEY NEW DELHI

An Imprint of Simon & Schsuter, Inc.
1230 Avenue of the Americas
New York, NY 10020

First Simon & Schuster trade paperback edition January 2024

SIMON & SCHUSTER PAPERBACKS and colophon are
registered trademarks of Simon & Schuster, Inc.

Simon & Schuster: Celebrating 100 Years of Publishing in 2024

For information about special discounts for bulk purchases,
please contact Simon & Schuster Special Sales at 1-866-506-1949
or business@simonandschuster.com.

The Simon & Schuster Speakers Bureau can bring authors to your live event.
For more information or to book an event,
contact the Simon & Schuster Speakers Bureau at 1-866-248-3049
or visit our website at www.simonspeakers.com.

Interior design by Ruth Lee-Mui

Manufactured in the United States of America

1   3   5   7   9   10   8   6   4   2

Library of Congress Control Number: 2022051122

ISBN 978-1-9821-9010-1
ISBN 978-1-9821-9011-8 (pbk)
ISBN 978-1-9821-9012-5 (ebook)

Contents

Preface

Who has impacted you on a deep, personal level and helped bring out your best? Maybe it was a parent, friend, or coworker. Maybe it was a celebrity, sports hero, or leader who inspired you to do greater things. For my coauthor, Michael Crom, and me, one of the most influential people in our lives was someone we've never met: Dale Carnegie, the author of *How to Win Friends and Influence People* and *How to Stop Worrying and Start Living* and the creator of the world-famous Dale Carnegie Course.

I remember my father talking about Dale when I was a teenager. My dad had a small den near our kitchen, and he sat me down one day for what appeared to be a serious conversation. "Joey," he said. "Life is about personal growth and building strong relationships. This book can help you as it has me." He handed me a fairly worn paperback copy of *How to Win Friends*. As I flipped through the tattered pages, I realized that my dad was a living example of the principles in this book. Everywhere we went, my dad greeted people with a broad smile and their name. He genuinely cared about the people he met.

Many years later, as a young lawyer, I decided to take a Dale Carnegie Course. Little did I know how that program would change the direction of my life. Inspired by what I had learned and filled with a renewed confidence and vision, I left the practice of law, went into business, and then started an e-learning company. Dale Carnegie Training became my first client. My company and I spent years developing online programs to reinforce what participants and graduates learned in the classroom. In building and selling my first company, surviving daunting challenges, and helping to start a second business, Dale's ideas were invaluable to me. His principles have helped me be a more attentive, caring, and supportive father, husband, friend, and leader. I attribute a tremendous amount of what I've achieved to Dale and his wisdom. Today, I have the privilege and honor of serving as the president and CEO of Dale's company, Dale Carnegie Training—a personal and professional training business, with two hundred operations in eighty-six countries, that strives to help people and teams unlock their greatness and perform at the highest levels.

Michael's story is a bit different since he is Dale's grandson. His childhood was a joyful one, growing up in a family that not only lived Dale's principles in business but applied them to their family's relationships. Michael's father, Ollie, joined Dale's company as a young man, working as a field trainer, and he ultimately became the organization's CEO.

"I admired my dad and always wanted to follow in his footsteps, but I was terribly introverted at the time. I was shy, unassuming, and uncomfortable being around other people. As a teenager, I could never envision myself as a trainer or leader as my father had been. But then I took the Dale Carnegie Course at fifteen, and it changed everything. All of a sudden, I had new tools that helped me be courageous and confident. It was like beginning a new stage of my life." Michael joined Dale Carnegie a year after graduating college. He worked as a shipping clerk, a software developer, an instructional designer, and eventually moved into sales and management roles around the United States. "I loved helping clients develop skills and tools that changed their lives for the better, just as the programs had changed my life." Michael eventually became the executive vice president and chief learning officer for Dale Carnegie Training. Today, he is active with his church and his community, and he serves on several boards, including Dale Carnegie's. While his most important role is as a father and husband, he finds great meaning and fulfillment in helping others realize their potential.

Who Was Dale Carnegie?

Dale was born on a farm in rural Missouri, where his parents struggled to survive. Year after year, the family faced misfortune—flooding that wiped out their crops, disease that killed their livestock, and crippling debt, which forced the family to sell their farm. Despite these challenges, Dale's family was loving and close. His parents, eager to help Dale and his brother, Clifton, experience an easier life, moved so the boys could attend a nearby teacher's college. It was there that Dale discovered his passion for public speaking as he joined debate and similar groups. Through hard work, Dale made a name for himself. After college, he decided to try his hand at sales, unsuccessfully at first, selling correspondence courses. He then moved to selling meat products, where he became the most successful salesperson in the country. Rather than joining management, he moved to New York City to follow his dream of becoming an actor. His acting career was not successful, so he experimented with several different jobs before he found his true purpose—teaching.

Through his work with his students, Dale realized how our fears, doubts, and worries can hold us back. He saw public speaking as a key to unlocking one's potential. In 1912, he created the Dale Carnegie Course, originally to help those with a fear of public speaking. He soon discovered that speaking was also a way to help people develop their human relations skills, which were a critical factor in their success.

Dale wrote *How to Win Friends and Influence People* after one of his students, a business manager for publisher Simon & Schuster, convinced him to do so. To Dale's great surprise and joy, it became an almost instant international bestseller. In fact, it was one of the top-selling nonfiction books of the twentieth century, selling an estimated sixty million copies. He later wrote another best-selling book, *How to Stop Worrying and Start Living*. The success of these books and his programs allowed Dale to begin developing Dale Carnegie Training as a global organization.

Dale's teachings became incredibly popular, and today, over 110 years later, millions of people around the world have taken one of Dale's programs, helping them achieve richer, fuller lives.

Why We Wrote *Take Command*

Michael and I owe a great debt to Dale for all that we have learned from him. We believe that when people implement his teachings, they can achieve personal growth, strengthen their relationships, and create the life they want. We are both passionate about helping people access this wisdom. We know that when we use these principles, we better our lives, our families, our work, and our communities.

If you've never encountered Dale Carnegie before, you might have an impression that these philosophies, and everything he stood for, relate solely to business. Although many people come through our doors because they've been sponsored by their company to attend a class, they soon realize that it's not all about work—that each principle applies to the rest of our lives, too.

We also know that many younger people aren't familiar with Dale. Even though Dale's wisdom is timeless, his stories from the early 1900s can be less relatable for some younger people. While Dale's principles apply now every bit as much as they did a hundred years ago, the world in which we live today is very different. The younger generations of the modern era face unique struggles. Living in a world that is ever more technologically connected and yet socially disconnected is not easy, and some of the seemingly basic concepts about how to live a good life have been lost. We believe today's generations need these philosophies for living more than ever.

With these things in mind, Michael and I set out to write *Take Command* to make this wisdom even more accessible to a younger generation. Living a principled, intentional life has impacted us powerfully and positively, and we hope it will do the same for you. We've interviewed hundreds of inspiring people from all over the world, and we're excited to share their stories with you. Michael personally interviewed close to one hundred people under thirty, all of whom have achieved impressive feats early in their lives. We've worked hard to include diverse stories from individuals of different ages, backgrounds, experiences, and walks of life. These people can inspire all of us to take command of our lives and futures.

We've organized this book into three parts. Think of it like three concentric circles, with Part I as the innermost circle and Part III as the outermost.

- **PART I: TAKING COMMAND OF YOUR THOUGHTS AND EMOTIONS**—We'll focus on how to build inner strength through understanding our thoughts and emotions and developing habits and practices to help us cultivate a strong, optimistic mindset. We'll talk about ways to handle stress, build courage and confidence, deal with change, and move past regret.
- **PART II: TAKING COMMAND OF YOUR RELATIONSHIPS**—Here we will explore our connections to the people we care about or interact with every day—how to establish and repair trust, deal with difficult people, sustain strong relationships, and see from another person's point of view.
- **PART III: TAKING COMMAND OF YOUR FUTURE**—In this section, we'll talk about defining your values, pursuing your purpose, and creating a vision for your life. We'll hear from some of the most incredible and inspiring young leaders around the world about how they pursue their dreams and make a lasting difference along the way.

This book is an invitation for you to take command of your thoughts, emotions, relationships, and future. If you simply read this book and say, "That was interesting," or "I really liked this book," but you do nothing, then we have failed. This book is not called *Learn* or *Study*. The book is called *Take Command*, encouraging you to do something. Practicing the ideas in this book is not merely an intellectual pursuit. To make this work, you have to first understand and then take action, try things out, and be willing to learn from any mistakes you make. Our goal is to equip you with powerful strategies *and* inspire you to live an intentional life.

Think of each principle as a tool. We use tools for specific purposes—you use a hammer to pound a nail, a saw to cut a board, and a screwdriver to tighten a screw. You can mix and match these concepts in a way that works for you. The more we use each principle, the more we understand how it works, and the better we'll get at it.

Dale said that knowledge isn't power. *Applied* knowledge is power. You can know all the right things to do, and yet if you don't do them, you're not going to receive the benefits that go along with them. Fulfillment is usually found outside of our comfort zone, not tucked safely within it.

When people are on their deathbeds talking about what they would have changed, many say, "I would have taken more risks," or "I would have been more intentional. My life just passed me by." If you want to get the most out of this book, you will read it, re-read it, and apply it again and again. The strategies we outline require ongoing attention and application. Our conviction is that if you focus on the right thoughts, work with your emotions, become more fearless and resilient, develop stronger and more meaningful relationships, and have the courage to pursue your passions, then you will be well positioned to take command of your future and your life.

Like Dale, Michael and I believe in the idea of "inherent greatness." This means that no matter who you are, what you do for a living, your intellectual capabilities, your socioeconomic group, or any other factor you can name, you have greatness within you. And if you choose to develop that greatness, there is no telling what you can do, achieve, or become. Perhaps more importantly, there is no limit to the difference you can make in the lives of others. The idea of inherent greatness is somewhat like the tip of an iceberg—the tip is only 10 percent of the actual iceberg. There is so much more to be discovered under the surface. The same is true for us when we develop our belief in ourselves, learn to treat other people with dignity and respect, and create a vision for what we want to achieve in life. Taking command means seeing and developing our inherent greatness so that we can live life to its fullest. We wish that for you as you begin this journey.

PART I

TAKING COMMAND OF YOUR THOUGHTS AND EMOTIONS

Taking command of our lives starts with facing our biggest potential obstacle: ourselves. Too often, *we* are the problem. We doubt our abilities; we allow ourselves to worry needlessly; we fail to take risks because we are afraid; we see ourselves as victims, instead of as people who have influence over our own destinies. All of these thoughts and emotions originate and exist in our minds, as does the ability to change them. But how do we do that? How do we form mindsets that empower us? How do we learn to manage our emotions so that they serve instead of undermine us?

In this section, we start with our thoughts and emotions—and how we can control them more effectively. While this might sound easy, it may be our greatest life challenge. Without the right framework and tools, we can easily drift from one negative thought or emotion to another.

While modern science has helped us understand our thinking patterns and emotional behaviors, we still don't have clear answers. Evolutionary theorists, noted psychologists, and philosophers all have different takes on which comes first—thoughts or emotions—and how they influence each other. And honestly, when we're in the middle of an argument with a friend, and our thoughts and emotions are running wild, does it really matter which theory we believe? No. What matters is that we learn to work with our thoughts and emotions and make decisions that move us toward the life we want.

We'll begin Part I by focusing on our thoughts, how they impact us, and how to choose the right ones. Then we'll look at routines that help us build a strong mindset. Next, we'll turn to our emotions, and we'll learn how to process them so we don't get lost in our feelings. Those first three chapters form the core of Part I. If you get only one thing out of this part, we hope that you gain a better understanding of what's happening in your head and your heart—and that you confront it.

Next, we'll look at building self-confidence, which affects the way we show up in the world—and impacts how we see ourselves and our abilities. Then we'll talk about embracing change. Change is the only constant in life, and most of us struggle to accept it. Finally, we'll explore how to move through regret, deal with stress, and build resilience and courage.

Our inner life—our thoughts, emotions, mindset, and reactions—are, to a large degree, under our control. We can choose one thought over another. We can change our minds. We can work with our emotions. We can build a mindset that supports us. We can cultivate strength and confidence and learn to deal with the unexpected and undesirable with wisdom and grace. Your inner life is yours to command.

1

CHOOSE YOUR THOUGHTS

I now know with a conviction beyond all doubt that the biggest problem you and I have to deal with—in fact almost the *only* problem we
have to deal with—is choosing the right thoughts. If we can do that, we
will be on the highroad to solving all our problems.

—Dale Carnegie

March 2020. COVID-19 was spreading around the world, causing illness, death, and lockdowns. I was in my fifth year as Dale Carnegie's
CEO, and I watched helplessly as our offices around the world closed
one by one. Every night, I woke around 3 a.m. and could not fall back
asleep. Dark thoughts and worries consumed my mind. I feared the
107-year-old company I was leading might go out of business under my
leadership; I agonized over the stress our thousands of team members
around the world were under; I worried about my eighty-six-year-old
mother, who was living alone, hundreds of miles away; I dreaded thinking about friends, family, and people who might die. Days passed without my getting more than four hours of sleep. It was one of the lowest
points in my life.

Then one night when I woke, I had an idea. I picked up *How to Stop
Worrying and Start Living* and began flipping through it, looking for inspiration. This book had helped me handle stressful situations countless

times in the past. Why hadn't I thought to look at it earlier? I turned to the page with the quote that opens this chapter. In that moment, it was as though Dale himself were standing in my bedroom, talking to me personally. This was exactly what I needed to hear.

My thoughts had beaten me down for weeks, but now I finally stopped and really began thinking about them. I saw clearly how pessimistic and ugly they had been. Why had I allowed myself to be preoccupied with things that might never happen? Why was my mind turning to the worst possible outcomes? Why was I allowing myself to stew in this toxic negativity? Even though I knew better, I had allowed myself to be held hostage by fear—and it was ruining my sleep, health, and life.

I realized how my emotions had been so interwoven with my thoughts—I would think about horrible things that might happen, I'd feel sick with worry, and then the downward spiral would begin. Even though I believed deeply in Dale's stress and worry principles, I had forgotten them amid this crisis. I was dwelling on all of the potentially terrible outcomes and letting my thoughts and emotions run the show.

I thought to myself, "You know what, Joe? Your problem isn't with COVID-19. It's with your thoughts. Choose the right thoughts, and you'll get through this." It occurred to me, "What if I flipped this? Instead of dwelling on the pandemic and the things I can't control, why don't I focus on the things I can?" And then the eureka moment hit me: "If every action has an opposite and equal reaction, then with great crisis, there must be incredible opportunity. So, where is it here?"

Before the pandemic, we had already started transitioning our company's global training program from almost entirely in-person to online, which was no easy feat given that we had thousands of employees in two hundred operations in over eighty countries. What if we could accelerate that transition? How could we double or triple our efforts to make this initiative successful? And how could I better support our Dale Carnegie customers, leaders, and employees around the world who also faced anxiety about everything that was happening? How could I build them up? My mood began to change. I was getting excited about taking command, making things happen, leading our company through this crisis, and finding a way to thrive during the pandemic. I remembered the advice a wise friend shared with me. Early in my career, I was hesitant to make a move because I was afraid a bad economy would hurt the business I'd be joining. My friend said, "Remember, Joe, the stormy sea makes a skilled sailor, not a smooth one. You grow and become better through hard times." Then I thought, "These are extraordinarily hard times, and if I respond well, I will become a stronger leader. How many people have had the opportunity to lead a 107-year-old company through a crisis like this one? I am standing in Dale's shoes. I owe it to him and to everyone to lead with confidence, not cowardice. What would Dale do?" Over the months that followed, I watched with awe and gratitude as we came together as one unified company with courage and flipped our entire business model from in-person to online delivery.

I also thought about what I could do to support my family and friends. Yes, I was probably more of a nag with my mother during our nightly FaceTime calls about staying safe, but she appreciated it. I reached out to friends and colleagues around the world to check in, listen, and remind them of how important they were to me. I made even more time for my wife and kids, which wasn't hard since we were locked in the same house together 24/7, but I was more intentional about our time together. I began to exercise more, eat better, eliminate refined sugar from my diet, take vitamins, and do all I could to help build my immune system in case I got COVID-19.

That night was one of the most pivotal of my life, and I will be forever grateful for it. Dale's quote reminded me about the critical importance of my thoughts. I had to pay attention and be active with them. I needed to choose empowering thoughts that led me to action instead of destructive ones that dragged me into darkness and despair, spurring me into passivity. I realized that if I chose the right thoughts, I would be on the "highroad to solving" all of my problems. And if I failed to do this, I would remain in a very bad place mentally and emotionally. I saw that everything in our lives—relationships, careers, goals, health, achievements, etc.—depends on the first step of taking command of our thoughts. The good news, and the purpose of this chapter, is to show that if you do this, you can have incredible peace, confidence, and inner strength in any situation, too. Now, let's talk about how.

Pay Attention to Your Thoughts

How often do you think about what you think? I mean *really* think about the thoughts in your mind. Most of us go from thing to thing, conversation to conversation, class to class, meeting to meeting, reacting to things that happen to us. We read an email that sets us off; we see a social media post that annoys us; we find something online that makes us laugh; someone wrongs us, and we're ready to fight. When this happens, how often do we stop and say, "Hold on, am I really thinking about this the right way? How am I seeing this?"

Too often, our mind is on autopilot. We might hear the words in our heads, "I can't do that," and we accept that thought as fact. We don't stop to examine or challenge that thought; we just accept it and keep moving. We don't even try. Or maybe we have a strong opinion about a person. We perceive that we are threatened, disliked, or judged because our thoughts tell us so, and we don't stop even for a moment to consider if we could be seeing things incorrectly.

My longtime friend Emma stopped by my house recently to visit our family. She was telling me about how she was struggling with a colleague, Julie, who had recently joined her department, and who Emma said was condescending. "What happened, Emma? Why do you feel that way?" I asked.

"I handle the creative work for all our social media campaigns, and that includes developing images and key messages for our posts. I've done this for years, and I'm good at it. So I'm talking with Julie, and she starts making suggestions about how I could do my creative work better. Who does she think she is? I know how to do my job!"

"Did she actually criticize your work or say it was bad?" I asked.

"No. It wasn't that. She was just asking me questions. 'Have you ever considered changing this color from yellow to light blue? Or making that image a bit bigger? Or have you ever tried a different font?' Those types of questions," Emma said.

"Was she giving you attitude, or did she have a critical tone? Any eye rolls?"

"No, she didn't," Emma shot back. "None of that. But I could just tell she didn't like my design and thought she could do it better."

"Emma," I said, "is it possible that Julie was just trying to help you? Maybe she was trying to contribute to making your social media posts even better. What is the thought you are telling yourself about Julie?"

"Well," Emma said, "The thought is that she doesn't think I know what I'm doing."

"Okay, you could be right, but how do you know what's in her mind? I can think of many times I've tried to help someone at work by suggesting ways to improve. I wasn't trying to put them down. Why not assume that Julie has positive intent? Given everything you've said, I think she was trying to help you."

Emma looked at me, said, "Whatever," and abruptly walked away—every bit as upset and convinced she had been wronged as when she first sat down with me. Sometime later, after talking with my wife, Katie, about the same thing, Emma came back and said, "You know, I've been thinking about what you said, and it's possible I'm wrong about her. Julie doesn't seem like a bad person. In fact, she's actually been pretty friendly. Maybe it was how she said it that rubbed me the wrong way, or maybe she just got me at a bad time. Honestly, I wasn't having the best day when we talked. I was definitely irritable going into the conversation. As soon as the thought came into my mind that Julie was criticizing me, I tensed up and got pretty defensive. Maybe I should give her the benefit of the doubt."

We give meaning to the things that happen in our lives through our thoughts, and, for better or worse, that meaning affects how we think, feel, act, and react. We all know people who are miserable no matter what happens to them. They could be in a healthy relationship but worry irrationally that their significant other will leave them. They could be promoted at work but complain about all the additional responsibility. We also know people who somehow remain unfazed and cheerful in a horrible situation. It doesn't matter what life throws at them; they have a positive outlook. Why is that? What is the difference between these two types of people? The difference comes down to how we think.

If we tend to think negatively, we might feel threatened or hopeless. If we tend to think optimistically, we might see opportunities others do not and be more confident about the future. Whatever we think, it impacts everything. The Roman philosopher Marcus Aurelius said that "Our life is what our thoughts make it."[1] For most of us, the challenge is that we are hardly aware of our thoughts and the life they create. We know the thoughts are there, but do we think about how we limit ourselves by focusing on bleak, fearful, or irrational worries? Do we know how our thoughts can lead us to feel angry, frustrated, or resentful? We have to take command of our thoughts, or they will take command of us. That's just reality. But how do we do that?

It all starts with paying attention to the way we think. Here's a challenge: The next time you find yourself with a strong thought pattern or emotion—write it down and observe it. Ask yourself a few questions:

- "What are the thoughts I'm having, and how do I experience them?" Some people hear an inner voice, while others think in pictures and impressions. Notice how your thoughts occur to you in that moment.
- "How are those thoughts causing me to feel?"

- "Am I making assumptions here—putting words in people's mouths, or taking the situation out of context?"
- "Is this a helpful thought? If not, what can I replace it with?"

Ralph Waldo Emerson is reported to have said, "A man is what he thinks about all day long." How could we be anything else? The ideas that you take in are like the food that you eat—just like any meal, you have to digest them. Every movie you watch, book you read, and social media feed you scroll through influences your thoughts.

How and with whom you spend your time will impact your thoughts, and it's important to pay attention to the influences in your life. For a brief time, I studied stand-up comedy, and while I waited for my turn, I watched other comedians and listened to their routines. Some of their jokes were so vile they left me nauseated—their ideas affected me. It might have taken a couple of days to get that junk out of my head. Sometimes, we have to look at our lives and rethink the people we hang out with and the things we do if they influence our thoughts negatively.

Seeing our thoughts honestly, whether that happens in a sudden aha moment or over time, helps us understand how they shape our lives. That clarity helps us choose to think differently, to adopt a different attitude about the problems we are facing. Choosing the right thoughts can be tough, and for some of us, it might be the greatest challenge we face. Although it can be hard at first, our thinking habits are the foundation for taking command of our lives. When we can consistently avoid negativity and choose thoughts that serve us, we are on the path to a healthy mindset that will help us succeed.

Why We Dwell on Negative Thoughts

Unfortunately, we are wired to think negatively. Early humans had one goal: survive. If they were always watching for danger, they could outrun hungry carnivores. Every day was a fight for food, so they couldn't trust anyone outside of their nomadic tribes. Paying attention to danger helped them stay alive longer and pass on their genes. In other words, our instinct to dwell on negative thoughts is our brain's way of keeping us safe. This is called negativity bias.[2]

What that means is we tend to remember sad or traumatic events more than positive ones. Insults are etched into our memories, but we struggle to remember compliments. We naturally assume the worst in almost every situation. When our boss asks to meet with us, our first inclination might be "Did I do something wrong?" On an impulse, I called a friend I hadn't talked to in years just to say hello, and his first question was "Is everything okay?" He thought I might be calling to deliver bad news. This natural bias toward the bad affects our decision-making, too.[3]

Many times, these thoughts start with "I can't," "I shouldn't," or "I couldn't," and are followed with "because," and a self-defeating reason. Let's look at some examples of limiting thoughts below. As you read these, ask yourself, "Which of these, if any, apply to me?"

- "I am a failure unless I do everything perfectly." This is an example of extreme thinking—when we see things as all or nothing, as if we will either succeed or fail, win or lose, without acknowledging the gray areas in between.
- "I can't ask that person out. They'll say no and laugh at me." We call this focusing on imminent disaster. When we believe that disaster lurks around every corner, a single unwelcome event or piece of criticism can ruin our week.
- "I messed up my presentation, and I'll probably get fired." When we magnify the negative and focus more on our mistakes than on areas of good performance, we overblow the reality of the situation. Other examples include being unreasonably hard on yourself because you got a B+ on your exam when you're used to

getting an A or punishing yourself because you said "the wrong thing" in a conversation with someone you care about.

- "I should've gotten more done, and I didn't." When we overemphasize "should" and compare ourselves to the ideal, we will always come up short. We berate ourselves for "failing," even if we had legitimate reasons for not completing our to-do list—even if that list was unrealistic in the first place.
- "I'm an idiot, and it's all my fault." When we box ourselves into a nonrational thought process, we make ourselves miserable. There is nothing objectively true about the statement, but because we might be frustrated or emotionally depleted, we believe these negative thoughts.
- "It's not my fault. I'm the victim." Unlike the prior limiting thoughts, where we blame ourselves for everything, in this case, we blame ourselves for nothing. Someone else is always responsible if something goes wrong. This belief—even if true—can disempower us and make us feel helpless. It's not where we want to be.

Now, Michael and I are not saying that we don't face real tragedy and injustice. We do. Very bad things do happen. And no one is saying we should wear blinders and deny the challenges before us. We shouldn't. What we are saying is that even in the worst situations, we can decide what we will think—and those decisions will shape our action or inaction. If we dwell too long on the tragedies we encounter, we may never move on; and if we don't move on, we may miss so much that is wonderful in life.

This is where the power to choose comes in. Yes, we may be wired to think a certain way, but that doesn't mean we don't have any control over our thoughts. When we practice paying attention to our thoughts, we become attuned to how each one affects us, determine whether it's helpful in the given situation, and proceed with a thought that's more encouraging.

Not long ago, a large nonprofit organization asked Michael to give a keynote talk. When he said yes, he felt good about it. But as the event approached, Michael regretted it: "Why in the world did I say yes to this? I just don't see this going well. I've never given a talk on this topic to a group like this. And why did they ask *me* to do this? They should have picked a better speaker." As soon as Michael noticed these thought patterns, he stopped himself and said, "Wait a second. I've given hundreds of talks. Most have gone really well. This organization picked me for a reason. What do I need to do to show them and myself that they made the right decision?" Michael dug into preparing. He researched the group and committed to being twice as prepared as he might normally be. When the emcee introduced him to speak, Michael looked at the audience, smiled, and began his talk with sincere, heartfelt energy. At one point, he could hear his inner voice saying, "This is going wonderfully! I should do this more often!" As he thought this, he felt a renewed energy and a great connection with his audience. In that moment, he knew he wanted to give more talks in the future. Organizers told Michael his talk was one of the most inspiring they had ever had. Michael says he never would have succeeded that day if he hadn't shut down the undermining thoughts and replaced them with empowering ones.

Choosing the Right Thoughts

Choosing constructive thoughts can be difficult, especially when we're facing circumstances that feel hopeless. But overcoming discouraging thoughts can be as simple as shifting how we think—and we can start right now. When choosing better thoughts, remember these three strategies—and we encourage you to pick just one to work on at a time:

- Use negative thoughts as an early warning system
- Reframe your thoughts
- Practice affirmations

Use Negative Thoughts as an Early Warning System

Sometimes, negative thoughts can serve us, much like a blinking "oil low" light on your car dashboard does. We're not happy to see that light go on, but we're grateful because it tells us that if we don't do something, we're going to have an even bigger problem. We can use negative thoughts and emotions the same way—as soon as we become aware of them, we can stop and ask, "What is this thought or feeling telling me? What do I need to do now to stop this situation from escalating?"

As the CEO and cofounder of Pillar Technologies, Alex Schwarzkopf put tremendous pressure on himself to perform well. His company developed risk management technology for contractors to use at construction sites, and it was a big job. After months of working sixty-plus-hour weeks, responding to late-night emails, and working with his team on bug fixes, the chaos was starting to eat at him, and he knew something had to change.

Alex started to pay closer attention to what he was thinking and feeling. He noticed that he often entertained negative thought loops: one focused on his self-worth ("I'm just not any good at this. I'm in way over my head"), and the other reinforced his harsh self-judgment ("I am just the worst. I can't do anything right"). He compared himself to others who seemed to have more—success, money, friends—even though his life was objectively very good.

After observing the thought loops, he realized, "I'm literally creating this as I go. Those stories, those thoughts, are making me anxious—and I know they're not true," he said. Like so many of us, Alex had fallen into the habit of believing his negative thoughts were true when, in fact, they were false narratives he made up about himself and other people. That's when negative thoughts are most dangerous—when we put too much stock in them. They affect not only our decisions but our moods, too. Breaking the cycle requires that we stop living out these negative stories and act from a place of empowerment.

In Alex's case, self-defeating thoughts caused him to feel depressed. He experienced burnout twice before he realized he needed help. "I knew I didn't want to feel that way and that I needed to do something about it," Alex said. He went on a retreat to reset his body and mind, and when he got back, he spent eighteen months doing different types of therapy to get to the root of his negative thought patterns. Through that work, he acquired a few tools to help him recognize those unhelpful patterns.

Now, as soon as he begins to feel anxious, Alex treats it as though sirens are wailing and red lights are blinking. One morning, Alex woke up feeling worried and down. In the past, this might have derailed his entire day, but because he had learned to view his anxiety as an early warning sign, he pulled his team together. Instead of ruminating on the thought, Alex shared what he knew about the customer-related problem that was bothering him and asked for help in dealing with it. In minutes, the group helped him develop a solution, which immediately eased his anxiety. The more he practiced noticing his negativity bias and taking action, the more confident he felt that he could shake a negative thought pattern. Just like dwelling on negative thoughts can create a downward spiral, focusing on positive thoughts can create an uplifting, self-assuring cycle.

The next time you perceive a negative thought, consider it a warning sign. First, stop and challenge yourself. Ask, "What is this thought telling me?" Then ask yourself, "What do I need to do now?" Decide what action you need to take to alleviate the warning sign.

Reframe Your Thoughts

Another way to choose the right thoughts is to rework them—take the negative thought and say, "How might I see this as something that can help me?"

Artis Stevens was a star football player in high school who dreamed of playing at the University of Georgia. He trained for years, and he was completely committed to this goal. He was highly recruited, but, unfortunately, he suffered a devastating leg injury. He received medical advice that, based on this injury, he would not be able to play football at the same level again.

"When I heard that," Artis said, "It was like watching my dream go up in smoke."

Artis experienced depression. His friends, family, and community came together and helped him see that, in the long run, doing well in football wasn't as important as doing well in school. They challenged his vision for himself and encouraged him to look at his situation in a new way. "The turning point for me was changing my thoughts and my definition of success. I told myself that success meant winning on the football field. But when I changed what success meant to me, that it was about being more aligned with my purpose, I realized all of my previous work wasn't for nothing—I could use the same skills I had developed to achieve athletically in my academics. I started viewing all my hard work as practice for my next challenge." When Artis got into the University of Georgia based on academics and not athletics, it was an affirmation that he had taken the right approach. "I always knew that I had to work incredibly hard to get to where I was, and the idea of achieving my dreams was still achieving my dreams—it was just achieving them in a different way."

Once Artis redefined how he thought about success, that opened up entirely new possibilities. He not only excelled in college and graduated, but he also rose quickly in his career. Today, Artis is the president and CEO of Big Brothers Big Sisters of America, and he is bringing that same insight to the organization. Challenging and reframing your definitions of success and failure can be a critical way to take command and live the life you truly want.

We will all experience many moments in our life where we have to reframe the way we think about a given situation. It won't always be about success and failure—maybe we'll have to rethink how we see an opportunity or how we think about a relationship. Reframing our thoughts is a skill we must practice over the course of our lives. So what are some ways we can reframe our thoughts? Here are a few ideas:

- First, be clear about what you are thinking. In Artis's case, he believed that success in life depended on success in football. You can't reframe your thoughts until you know what they are.
- Second, challenge the thought. Ask yourself, "How else could I see this?" Consider the alternative. If Artis's belief was "My success depends on football," he could say, "My success does not depend on football," and add the word "because" at the end. "My success does *not* depend on football because . . ." and then think about some reasons that could follow the statement, such as "My success does not depend on football because my life is more than just a sport. I have many other talents. I am smart, hardworking, and tenacious. I can contribute to my friends and family."
- Third, do one thing in support of the statement you've just made. It doesn't have to be big, but do something—even one thing can lead to the next thing and create momentum. Using Artis's example, he might have asked a friend or family member about the talents they saw in him; he might have gone online to check the academic requirements for the University of Georgia; he might simply have written the statement above so he could look at it. Again, it doesn't matter what the action is as long as it pushes you in a new, productive direction.

Reframing your thoughts can be like building a muscle—the more you do it, the stronger you become. Practice this technique the next time you notice a self-limiting belief or negative thought, and you will witness how reframing can begin to change everything.

Practice Affirmations

Most people are familiar with the term *affirmations*—these have been around for a long time, and there is a reason for that: they work. Stated simply, an affirmation is a word or phrase you say repeatedly to reinforce a belief you want to have.[4] Doing this conditions the mind, much like lifting weights builds muscle. Affirmations are a way of strengthening the thoughts you want to think and rebutting the thoughts that hold you back. We believe everyone should use them.

When choosing our affirmations, there are a few key things to remember. First, we need to have faith in the affirmation we say to ourselves. If we don't believe what we're saying is possible, the affirmations won't work. Second, affirmations should be written and spoken in the present tense, as if what we want is already happening. Third, avoid using "negative" affirmations. For example, if we were inclined to say, "I will stop feeling anxious," we might instead choose to say, "I am calm and peaceful." Finally, use affirmations every day to get the most out of them. Just like we must work out regularly and eat well at each meal to be healthy, we must also have a daily practice that includes our affirmations.

Here are a few examples of affirmations to consider:

- "I am strong and capable of achieving what I want in life."
- "Every day, I improve and get better."
- "I am powerful."
- "Everything I need to succeed I already have within me."

You can even simplify your statement down to one word. For many years, Michael picked a single word that he focused on for a full year—words such as *enthusiasm*, *action*, *joy*, *discipline*. We can even create affirmations for people we love.

When Camille Chang Gilmore's sons were four and five, they were both diagnosed with autism spectrum disorder. When she heard the diagnosis, Camille felt so devastated that she went into her closet, fell on her knees, and cried, thinking, "Why me?" After allowing herself a moment to grieve, she acknowledged her negative thoughts and reminded herself that this wasn't about her. It was about her boys, and it was time to get to work.

Camille got out of her head and took steps to help her sons. Camille found the best medical care they could receive and made sure the boys had good tutors. But perhaps the most important thing Camille did was to share an affirmation with them. Every day, she said, "You are . . . ," and they responded, "Destined for greatness!" The boys shouted this at the top of their lungs throughout their childhood.

Camille's boys are now in their twenties and both at universities. With the encouragement of their mother, the support of tutors, and access to the right accommodations, their confidence and self-assurance have led them to succeed. Camille worked hard not to let her negative thoughts overtake her, and she coached her boys to be positive.

If your dream is to inspire people, then you might tell yourself, "I inspire others to live their best lives." Use active words as often as you can when building your affirmations. The words should resonate with you.

Do you have written affirmations? If not, Michael and I challenge you to stop reading right now, define one affirmation that fills you with confidence, write it down, and start saying it at least five times a day, once in the morning and at night and at least three other times. I try to do this every day and have for years. Affirmations are a key part of taking command, increasing confidence, and becoming resilient.

TAKE
COMMAND

Paying attention to our thoughts and learning to work with them is a lifelong practice. We must make the daily commitment to be aware of and actively choose thoughts that help us build the life we want. If we do that, as Dale said, we "will be on the highroad to solving all our problems."

PRINCIPLE

Choose empowering thoughts.

ACTION STEPS

- **PAY ATTENTION TO YOUR THOUGHTS.** Starting right now, take some time to notice your thoughts. What becomes apparent when you pay attention? Are your thoughts harmful or supportive? Do you tend to see the worst in every situation, or do you look for the best? What patterns do you see?
- **NOTICE YOUR LIMITING THOUGHTS.** Review the list above and notice the kinds of negative thoughts you have. Do you catastrophize? Do you magnify the negative? How does that make you feel when you slip into those thought patterns? What would happen in your life if you changed those thoughts to something that served you?
- **PRACTICE CHOOSING THE RIGHT THOUGHTS.** This is a daily challenge—it's not

a solution you try once. You must practice this every day to build the muscle. The more you practice, the stronger you'll get.

- **USE NEGATIVE THOUGHTS AS AN EARLY WARNING SYSTEM.** When you notice a negative thought, think about what it might indicate to you. Is there something in your life that is troubling you?
- **REFRAME YOUR THOUGHTS.** Choose a different way to look at the situation. Ask yourself, "How could I see this a different way?"
- **PRACTICE AFFIRMATIONS.** Come up with uplifting statements that you can use to strengthen the thoughts you want to have.

2

CONDITION YOUR MIND
FOR SUCCESS

If you are not in the process of becoming the person you want to be, you are automatically engaged in becoming the person you don't want to be.

—Dale Carnegie

In my thirties, I came across a quote from the legendary baseball player Mickey Mantle that jolted me to action: "If I had known I was going to live this long, I'd have taken better care of myself." In that moment, I saw myself decades into the future as an older, unhealthy person who regretted his earlier choices about diet and exercise. I was never very athletic, but I couldn't use that as an excuse. So I started running to get fit. It was one of the hardest things I ever did.

At first, running was miserable. I struggled to go even a few miles, I had to stop often, and my legs and lungs hurt. I felt terrible. I dabbled in extreme thinking—a very clear and assertive voice in my mind kept saying, "QUIT! You're never going to be able to do this." I probably would have listened to that negative thought if it hadn't been for a good friend, Eric Eder, who encouraged me to push through those tough times. As a side note, we all need good friends to keep us on track sometimes.

I remember how thrilled I was to run six miles for the first time, then eight, then twelve. What seemed impossible started to become a reality. It was then that Eric suggested we run the Toronto Scotiabank Marathon. While that would have been unthinkable in the beginning, now that I could run twelve miles, I figured, "What's another fourteen?" (a not-so-bright idea in hindsight . . .).

To run a marathon, I knew I needed more than just persistence and a willingness to ignore my negative thoughts and discomfort. I needed a plan and a routine. I hired a coach who said that training for a marathon was different than going out for a run. I would have to condition myself in very specific ways. This involved twelve weeks of regimented training (running six days a week, including intense speed work on a track, consistent fast "tempo" runs, weekly long runs, and three easy pace runs), together with proper nutrition, rest, and hydration. My coach said, "I won't kid you. This is going to require consistency—monthly, weekly, daily, hourly—but if you stick with the plan, you'll be fine." I did. I followed my coach's plan religiously, and I ran my first marathon in just under three and a half hours. I could barely walk, but I didn't care. It was exhilarating.

Just as running a marathon requires consistent training over time, so, too, we need to condition our minds for success. We need a plan, and we need to stick with it. While it's great to reframe our thoughts or practice affirmations once or twice, we want to get to a place where this becomes habitual and automatic—where, whatever happens in our lives, we can face it instinctively with confidence, courage, and resilience. In other words, we want to develop mindsets that serve us, which we will discuss more later in this chapter. One powerful way to do that is to build routines that help us be our best on a daily basis.

Use Routines to Condition Your Mind for Success

A routine, as we define it, is a series of growth-oriented practices that lead to the development of a healthy mindset. Routines are not just a "nice to have" in life; they are a "must have." Having some sort of structure to your day cuts down on the number of decisions you have to make, which decreases stress, increases focus, and gives you an overall sense of peace and stability. Humans have been practicing routines for hundreds of years—Benjamin Franklin, Maya Angelou, T. S. Eliot, Mozart, Jane Austen, and Pablo Picasso all had routines. Ben Franklin would rise around 4 or 5 a.m., bathe, and eat breakfast. He would prepare for the day, asking himself, "What good shall I do this day?" and then begin his work by 8. At noon, he would break for lunch and read while eating (which lasted for two hours). After lunch, he'd resume his work until 6 p.m. He would rest and relax from then on, during which time he might enjoy a cold "air bath"—sitting next to an open window nude until 9 or 10, when he turned in for the night. Before he fell asleep, he would revisit the question from that morning and answer, "What good have I done today?"[1]

A more contemporary example is international best-selling author Haruki Murakami. He wakes up at 4 a.m. and writes for five to six hours. Then he runs or swims (or both), reads, and listens to music. He goes to bed at 9 p.m. Murakami said, "I keep to this routine every day without variation. The repetition itself becomes the important thing; it's a form of mesmerism. I mesmerize myself to reach a deeper state of mind."[2] Routines will differ across generations and continents, but the core motivation is the same: to set ourselves up for success in mind, body, and spirit.

Routines boost our mental health by helping us manage anxiety and stress. Part of this comes from the focus on things we can control. Routines add structure and create predictability in the day or week, especially during times of high stress. They also give a sense of accomplishment when we complete them. Sports psychologists note that pregame rituals lead to better performance and less anxiety.[3]

If we don't take time to design a routine that helps us condition our minds, our day and our thoughts will be dictated by events and circumstances. Like the frame of our house, our routines are the structure on which the rest of our day hinges.

Life without a Routine

If you met Michael today, you'd think he was the kindest person you'd ever met. But when he talks about who he was in his twenties, he admits that he was constantly trying to prove himself and had a bit of a temper when pushed. He worked hard—maybe a little too hard—and didn't yet understand the value of rest (which we will talk about in Chapter 7, "Deal with Stress"). He was driven to make a name for himself. That was okay, except that it led him to a life that was out of balance. His friend group was not the best influence, and he did not have a routine—he ran from appointment to appointment and worked long, stressful hours. He had no time built into his day for reflecting on or working with his emotions, not to mention thinking about the kind of life he wanted to build. "The lack of routine meant that I did not have space to take stock of my mindset. I had no time to either prepare or review my day," Michael said. As a result, he often felt backed up against a wall and emotionally reactive.

At one point, Michael managed a regional Dale Carnegie team, and one of the top salespeople in the world worked for him—"Fred" was number two at the company in personal sales. With a résumé like that, Michael convinced himself he needed Fred, and Fred picked up on that. He started ordering Michael around—and he even took a two-week vacation to the Caribbean on a day's notice. "If he hadn't been producing 80 percent of my business, and if I hadn't been a twenty-five-year-old kid who was nervous and unsure of himself, I would have fired him," Michael said. But Michael was busy trying to prove himself, he lacked confidence, and he simply reacted to life the best he could. One day, things came to a head when Fred came charging into his office, screaming at Michael about losing a large sale. Michael was so close to hitting him that he told Fred to back out of his office and not to come back with this attitude.

This experience was an epiphany for Michael. He said, "As a twenty-five-year-old, I wasn't equipped—mentally or emotionally—for this guy. I realized I needed to do something to improve myself, or I'd struggle with the next Fred. I knew I wouldn't grow in my career if I didn't become more confident and able to handle people better." Michael considered what he needed—space to think about and plan for his day, and to make decisions about how to work with the people around him. He began a daily practice of setting aside time to reflect on what was going well and what needed improvement, and to think about how he could make himself a better leader. He also adopted the practice of writing a mission statement for himself (which we'll go over in Part III). In his mission statement, he described in detail the kind of person he wanted to be: he wanted to use his gifts and talents to make a significant difference in people's lives. Michael's statement also affirmed that he was in control of his thoughts and emotions so that he could be a positive leader in his organization. "I carried that statement with me everywhere, and I looked at it every day. That statement became a critical part of my new daily routine, which included positive affirmations and setting aside time to reflect and plan prior to work. This new routine helped me enormously and continued to for decades. I became the person I described in my mission statement—and I became much better at handling difficult people and situations."

Build a Routine

For a long time, Jéssika Santiago knew she should make healthier choices, but life always got in the way. She wanted to exercise more but never had the energy because she prioritized work over everything else. She wanted to eat healthier food, but she didn't have time to cook. Although she was stressed out enough to notice that her body didn't feel good, she couldn't change—until her health really started to suffer.

Jéssika's doctor was direct: "You have an infection for which there is no medication. The only way you can heal this is by living a healthier, more balanced life." On top of that, Jéssika found out that she was pre-diabetic because of the way she was eating. This was a loud wakeup call that something had to change.

Jéssika knew she couldn't do it alone, so she asked a friend to help. The first thing they did was sit down and create a plan to improve the way Jéssika ate. "We talked about the things I enjoyed eating and decided that we wouldn't make radical changes and cut out the things I like, but we would work on building in one healthy thing at a time," she said. She started by setting up a morning routine that made it easy for her to eat a healthy meal as soon as she woke up. She set her alarm at the same time every day, so she created a natural sleeping rhythm. After a few weeks of settling into that routine, she incorporated exercise by going for a walk immediately after she ate.

The bonus of having a morning routine became apparent less than two weeks in. "When I woke up, I did not have to think about what time to start my day, and because I was no longer as tired as I used to be, I stopped hitting the snooze button repeatedly," Jéssika said. The routine meant that everything was already decided, which eased her mind. With the routine, she didn't waste time or energy trying to "figure out" what her morning was going to look like because she already knew—and her routine supported her goal and newfound value of a healthy life. "Those small decisions that I took off my plate made a huge difference. I had no idea how much time, mental space, and energy those decisions took up," she said.

Jéssika felt completely different after incorporating her routine. It was like flexing and strengthening a new muscle, which helped her build confidence and believe that she could do it. "It wasn't just what I was doing—eating healthy and exercising. The most important part was the confidence I felt. I had been telling myself that I needed to exercise for the past three or four years, and I had never been able to do it," she said. "It helped me build a better mindset because I started to believe that I could do hard things. When I dealt with other challenges in life, I started to think, 'Oh, I've got this. I can do it. If I go one step at a time, I am capable of growing and changing.' "

One of the most important things we teach in our Dale Carnegie Course is the importance of living an intentional life. While we will discuss this idea in depth in Part III, we want to highlight now that creating and following healthy routines are critical parts of living an intentional life. The difference between having or not having a routine can truly be like the difference between a boat that does or does not have a rudder. Self-care that includes our mind and body increases our energy, keeps our attitude positive, and helps us manage stress. Making time to reflect and plan for the day ultimately helps us become the people we want to be.

Create a Growth Mindset

Michael and Jéssika used routines not just to improve their lives but to create a new mindset—one which helped them become more confident, resilient, and capable of dealing more effectively with others. When they faced challenging situations, their reactions were not just positive—they were automatic. Stanford psychologist and researcher Carol Dweck wrote about this in her groundbreaking book *Mindset*. Whether we are aware of it or not, we all have a certain way of seeing the world. Dweck wrote that people with a "fixed" mindset believe that abilities, intelligence, and personality are set in stone and cannot be changed. This is the view that you're either born with skill, talent, or smarts—or you're not. In contrast, those who believe that our lives and abilities are flexible and can be shaped by learning and hard work have a "growth" mindset.[4]

We don't typically have one universal mindset. You might have a growth mindset in your job but also think that you will never be good at talking to people. In that case, you would have a growth mindset about your work and a fixed mindset about your social skills.

Whatever your mindset, it has a profound effect on your life. Research shows that those who have a growth mindset have more motivation and success. They also tend to have lower levels of anxiety, depression, and burnout.[5]

Forming a growth mindset approach to life is critical to our taking command—and it's one reason why having the right routine is so important. Having a routine that gives us time and space to think about and reflect on our thoughts, emotions, and experiences helps us choose our course of action. As you think about and build your routine, pay attention to thoughts that might tell you that you can or can't do something. Cultivating a growth mindset is possible, and it starts with paying attention to the way our thoughts affect us.

Start a Routine That Leads to a Growth Mindset

The purpose of building a routine is becoming the person you want to be—a healthier person, a patient parent, a compassionate teacher, a prolific writer, or someone who shows up on time—whatever is important to you. Your routine needs to fit your needs and life, so put the time into figuring out what routines will set *you* up for success.

My routine has developed over years. Most nights, I go to bed by 11 p.m. and wake at 6 a.m. I'm usually more alert, energetic, and creative in the morning, so I make the first forty-five to sixty minutes the foundation for my day. I avoid looking at my cell phone, which has been a huge derailer for me in the past. I've concluded that this is my focused time; emails, texts, and other messages can wait. I make a cup of hot green tea (though on some mornings, a more highly caffeinated beverage may be necessary) and go into a small room off the bedroom where I have a desk.

I meditate, reflect, pray, plan, and journal. I think about the previous day and ask myself, "What happened yesterday for which I'm grateful? What went well? Where was I effective?" I then move on to improvement: "What did not go as well as I'd have liked? Did I say or do anything that I need to fix today? If so, when am I going to do that?" For example, if I look at my interactions and decide that I was edgy or inconsiderate with someone, I'll talk to that person and make amends. I then review my personal vision and goals and think about the day ahead: "What are the critical things I must do today? When will I do that? How do I set myself up for success today?" Toward the end of my time, I'll write down in a journal any significant insights I've had. This routine gives me the time and space to think about my thoughts and actions and to plan while I am at my very best. It didn't just happen by itself—in the beginning, it was hard to get up and I was somewhat unfocused. But over time, it's become automatic.

A daily routine is not just a setup or an endpoint to the day. It serves as the gateway to a different way of thinking. When I finish my morning routine, I feel refreshed and focused and able to choose the direction for my day.

Sticking to a routine is a habit you have to build. To make progress, we have to not only avoid bad habits but consciously choose to build habits that positively affect our mental strength and clarity. Writer and researcher James Clear, author of *Atomic Habits*, has spent more than a decade searching out and writing on how to form positive habits. Clear says we should think about the following when we build new habits:

1. **START WITH A VERY SMALL HABIT.** We have a bigger chance of failing if we go for the hardest thing right away. For example, our goal shouldn't be "I will think only positive thoughts." That's going to be a very lofty goal to start with, and when we inevitably struggle, it will only lead us to feel discouraged. Instead, start with an easy habit—something like "I will say one positive affirmation every day."

2. **INCREASE YOUR HABIT IN A SMALL WAY.** One percent increases add up quickly. Build on your new habit in a small way every day. For example, after you've gotten into the habit of saying your affirmation, then add the practice of looking in the mirror while you do it. The next week, meditate on the affirmation for thirty seconds. Building on a habit in small ways helps keep the goal attainable and workable.

3. **SPLIT HABITS INTO CHUNKS.** Let's say you want to build the habit of meditation so that you can think more clearly and choose better thoughts. If you split the habit into two chunks, say ten minutes in the morning and ten minutes in the evening, the time commitment won't feel as heavy.

4. **WHEN YOU FALL OUT OF THE HABIT,** get back into it as quickly as you can. Everyone gets off track, even the best performers. Research shows that missing your daily habits once will not derail your long-term progress. The problem comes when we have an all-or-nothing mindset about our habits. If you miss a day and think, "Well, I broke my streak, and all of that was for nothing," you compound the problem. Accept that you will fall off track occasionally, and that's okay. Overall consistency is more important than perfection, so get back on track the very next day.[6]

Over time, my routine has changed as my life has changed, but the fact that I do it every day hasn't changed at all. Today, I can look at my day years or decades ago and see the change that has come from using a growth-oriented routine to build a healthy mindset. The time I've put into this gives me valuable perspective. It has helped me become mentally stronger, more confident and reflective, and, I hope, a kinder person.

The routine that works for me may not work for you. We all have different needs. Marie Kondo, author of *The Life-Changing Magic of*

Tidying Up, wakes up at 6:30 every morning, opens the windows to welcome the fresh air, and burns incense to purify her home. She likes to have a warm drink, then eat a simple breakfast with her husband and daughter. They will pray together, give thanks, and envision their ideal day. Marie likes to tidy her home before leaving for work and before going to sleep at night. While some routines show incredible discipline and dedication, not everyone has the luxury of time. Maybe you get exactly twenty minutes to yourself every day, from 5 p.m. to 5:20 p.m. You can use that time in a way that helps you reflect on the previous day or prepare for the next. Maybe you journal or meditate, exercise or stretch, or just sit quietly and think nothing.

Think about the routine you have now. Do you consciously decide on the activities you do every day, or do they just happen? Is your routine shaped by you or by the needs of other people? We all have families and obligations, but we want to challenge you to find a way to carve some time out for yourself every morning (or evening, if that works better) to engage in practices that help you build a constructive mindset.

It takes time and effort to create the kind of mindset that enables you to achieve what you want in life. You'll have to decide what works best for you over time, but we want you to challenge yourself—every day—with this set of questions:

- What's going well in your life? What are you grateful for? This helps you focus first on the things in your life that bring you joy, that you feel happy about.
- What's not going well? What parts of your life would you like to change? You might even rank these things to figure out where to start. The things you list should be specific points that you can improve. For example, instead of saying, "My relationship with my mother is struggling," you might say, "My relationship could benefit from more one-on-one time."

- What do you need to believe so you can improve the area that's most important to you? Let's say you're worried about how your relationship with your mother is going. It might be that the underlying belief behind that worry is that you won't be able to make it better. But to be able to make any kind of improvement in an area like this, you have to believe that you can have a close and connected relationship with your mother.
- What do you need to do to remind yourself of the new mindset? This is where you might use affirmations or take specific actions—like setting up a weekly meeting with your mom—to address the problem.

You can incorporate other constructive practices into your routine that will help you improve your mindset, like mindfulness, meditation, breathwork, prayer, journaling, or visualization. Exercise is also a great addition to a routine. The point is to make it work for you. Whatever practices you choose should help you become the person you want to be. Maybe you want to be more empathetic, proactive, ethical, responsible, generous, honest, calm, confident, or available. Choose a practice that guides you toward that goal.

A Note about Routines: Be Real

Remember, we create routines to serve us, not for us to serve them. In all likelihood, you will not be perfect, and you may get off track, but that doesn't mean you should feel guilty or bad about yourself. While trying to create or keep a routine, you might be traveling or on vacation; you may need to take care of a sick child in the middle of the night, or you may be ill yourself; you could go out with friends for a late night, have to work late, or face any number of situations that can derail your planned routine. That's life. What you don't want to do is to beat yourself up if you get off track for a legitimate reason. Cut yourself some slack and get back into your routine as soon as you can. Keep trying until you are successful, and don't give up. On the other hand, if you skip your routine because you're being lazy or making weak excuses, then disregard everything we've just said. It's time then to step up, take command, and make your routine happen.

TAKE COMMAND

It's not just about the routine itself, but about how the routine prepares us to achieve our goals and become the people we want to be. When we consciously decide how we will start, end, or live our day, and we build in practices that cultivate a strong mindset, we condition our minds for success. Doing that is key to living the life we want.

PRINCIPLE
Use supportive habits to develop your mindset.

ACTION STEPS

- **BUILD A ROUTINE.** Think about how you start your day. What practices do you do now that help you already? Do you meditate, journal, plan, pray, read, or exercise? How can you build on those helpful habits? If you notice that you don't have any helpful practices, what can you incorporate into your morning that will support you throughout your day?
- **MAKE A PLAN TO ADD SUPPORTIVE PRACTICES INTO YOUR DAY.**
  - Start with a small habit.
  - Increase it incrementally.
  - Split the habit into chunks.
  - If you fall out of the habit, get back into it quickly and don't beat yourself up about it.

- **USE THIS ROUTINE TO BUILD A GROWTH MINDSET.** Take out a pen and paper or use your favorite writing app. Ask yourself:
  - What's going well in your life? What are you grateful for?
  - What's not going well? What parts of your life would you like to change?
  - What do you need to believe so you can improve the area that's most important to you?
  - What do you need to do to remind yourself of your new mindset?
- **PAY ATTENTION TO YOUR MINDSET.** As you practice your routine, notice how it affects your mindset. How do you feel afterward? How do you feel when you skip it? How do you need to adjust your routine to achieve the mindset you want?

3

WORK WITH YOUR EMOTIONS

When dealing with people, let us remember we are not dealing with creatures of logic. We are dealing with creatures of emotion.

—Dale Carnegie

Deborah Ann Mack had been building her dry-cleaning business for almost a decade. She started with a pickup and delivery service in 2004, literally marketing door-to-door. Deborah went from zero customers to more than nine hundred in just a few years. Due to this growth, she hired several employees, and eventually built an organic dry-cleaning plant with an additional storefront to accommodate her business.

Deborah found a fixer-upper building to lease, but the landlord, who owned a construction business, blew the money she gave him for repairs. Now Deborah had a decrepit, broken-down building and a four-day route of clothes to clean. Instead of waiting around for the landlord to shape up, she scrounged up more money and started from scratch in a different rental space. She used all her money on the building, so she didn't have the funds to hire anyone to install or operate her dry-cleaning equipment. Deborah opened the instruction manuals, called her brother and some of his friends, and got to work.

By this time, Deborah was frustrated, angry, and anxious. She had put so much money into the business that she didn't feel she could quit. She had to make it work, as there was no other option.

With the equipment manufacturer's help, her brother and his friends were able to finish the construction. Things were finally moving ahead . . . until Deborah showed up at 5:30 one morning, like she always did, and opened the door to find a small ocean of water in her dry-cleaning plant. A pipe had burst. Deborah just stood there, frozen.

She grabbed an orange mop bucket, turned it over, and plunked herself down in the middle of the flooded room. Deborah felt defeated. She said to herself, "What else can go wrong? I'm in a flooded place. I'm trying to get this going. It's just one thing after another. We came here to rebuild and then the pipes and the property owners and . . ." Deborah was in despair.

She tried to cry. And she tried. And tried. She couldn't get a single tear to come out of her eyes. Then she started laughing—it struck her as funny that she was in the worst mess of her life, and she couldn't even shed a tear. She sat on that mop bucket and laughed until her stomach hurt and she couldn't breathe. She called her husband and, still laughing, said, "Honey, you won't believe it. The place is flooded. A pipe broke!" Her husband said, "Babe, why are you laughing?" And Deborah said, "Because it's funny!"

In a matter of minutes, Deborah's emotions went from shock, disbelief, despair, hopelessness, and frustration to surprise, joy, and freedom. She'd been working so hard for so many years that when she tried to give up, all she could do was laugh at how ridiculous her situation was. Every emotion came flooding out of her all at once, practically in the same breath. Deborah could have let her emotions run over. She could have bought into the feeling of failure and frustration and quit right then. But she knew that emotions come and go, and she knew how to work with them so that they benefitted her. She stood up from her bucket and got back to work, with renewed courage.

Once the plant was completed, Deborah hired counter help,

dry-clean pressers, and drivers for the pickup and delivery service. She never looked back because she knew failure was not an option. After owning the business for many years, she sold it and decided to return to college for fashion design. Today, she is the founder and designer of a luxury fashion brand, named after her.

You might not have a flooded dry-cleaning business on your hands, but we all struggle with tough emotions at times—body image issues might make us insecure or self-conscious; family conflicts can infuriate or frustrate us; friend group drama might leave us feeling isolated and worthless; chronic illness can exhaust and scare us. Life can be hard. But if we don't learn to manage our emotions, just like we did with our thoughts in Chapters 1 ("Choose Your Thoughts") and 2 ("Condition Your Mind for Success"), we will never be able to take command of our lives.

Think about a time in your own life when you were overcome with a negative emotion, when you felt powerless. Maybe you were angry, jealous, resentful, frustrated, afraid, or anxious. Maybe you're in that situation right now as you read this. What would it mean for you to break free of that emotion? What if you could learn to work with your emotions so that when you experience them, you still feel like you are in control? It's helpful to see our thoughts as passing clouds, and our emotions like storms that bring lightning and thunder. The sky doesn't cling to clouds or storms—it lets them come and go. That's what we're going to talk about in this chapter.

Why Do We Have Emotions?

Most researchers believe that emotions evolved to help us survive, reproduce, find food, and stay safe.[1] They impact the way we interact with the world. Emotions that we tend to label as "negative"—like sadness and anger—warn us and help us respond to or avoid a threat or a challenge. Sadness might show us that we need the company and care of the people around us, while anger might be a sign that someone has crossed a boundary and we need to address it. Those emotions have the effect of narrowing our focus so we can deal with the problem at hand. Emotions that we label as "positive"—like joy or empathy—help us widen our awareness and reveal opportunities and possibilities. They help increase our attention and memory, consider new ideas, and learn.[2]

Remember, our emotions can be just as negative or positive as our thoughts. There's a reason for that—just like our thoughts, emotions are difficult to understand. All of these processes are controlled by different parts of the brain (for example, the amygdala sorts and sends emotions to the prefrontal cortex, where they're handled appropriately).[3]

Researchers have identified at least five categories of emotion, including enjoyment, sadness, anger, fear, and disgust.[4] We might think of them as "pleasant" or "unpleasant," but they actually have a purpose:

1. **ENJOYMENT** describes the good feelings that come from familiar and new experiences.
2. **ANGER** is that driving fire when something stands in our way, or when we believe we're being treated unfairly.
3. **FEAR** lets us anticipate threats to our safety.
4. **DISGUST** allows us to know what doesn't feel right to us.
5. **SADNESS** comes as a response to loss. Feeling sad allows us to slow down and show others that we need support.

There are three parts to our emotional reactions: how we perceive the emotion, how our bodies experience the emotion, and how we act in response to the emotion.[5] In this chapter, we will learn to work with our emotions. We want to choose the way we act when we feel something. To do this, we're going to use a simple four-step process for seeing and understanding our emotions. Ask yourself:

1. How am I feeling?
2. What is the feeling telling me?

3. Is the feeling serving me?
4. How can I address this emotion and move forward?

Step One: How Am I Feeling?

Most of us struggle to identify or understand our emotions because we don't have the tools to do so. In her book *Atlas of the Heart*, author and research professor of social work Brené Brown describes how most people relate to their feelings: "What does it mean if the vastness of human emotion and experience can only be expressed as mad, sad, and happy? What about shame, disappointment, wonder, awe, disgust, embarrassment, despair, contentment, boredom, anxiety, stress, love, overwhelm, surprise, and all of the other emotions and experiences that define what it means to be human? . . . Language shows us that naming an experience doesn't give the experience more power, it gives *us* the power of understanding and meaning."[6]

Learning to describe our emotions helps us build greater resilience and self-awareness. After all, how can you work toward a solution if you can't name what's happening?

The next time you have intense feelings, take a moment to record the experience. Are you experiencing just one emotion or several? Can you name the emotions and their effect on you? Do this without judging or trying to fix them.

If the emotions feel too overwhelming and you don't want to write them out, try simply observing them. In the High Impact Presentation Course that we teach at Dale Carnegie, our participants each give a talk in front of the others. We record the talk, and as soon as they finish, the participant goes into the review room and watches the recording. Have you ever watched a recording of yourself talking? Like most of us, it might make you cringe. But here's the trick: the trainer tells the participant to watch as if they don't even know this person. Then the participant will ask themselves, "What is this person doing well? What aren't they doing? What is this person feeling while talking? What does their facial expression or body language say?" By stepping outside of ourselves for a moment, we can observe the cues we're giving and start to name our internal experience. It also helps to say things like "I notice that I'm feeling sad" instead of "I am sad." You are not your emotions, and you don't have to identify with them.

Another helpful way to start understanding your emotions is through psychotherapy. Thankfully, therapy is more accepted now than it was twenty years ago. Sometimes we're tempted to view therapy as a last resort for people who are dealing with intense trauma. But therapy is useful for anyone, in any stage of life, regardless of whether we "need it" or not. Working with a trained counselor can give you the dedicated space and time to unpack difficult emotions.

Step Two: What Is the Feeling Telling Me?

Even the hard emotions have something to teach us, so it's important that we work to understand them instead of hoping they'll go away. Edith Eger, a Holocaust survivor and psychologist specializing in post-traumatic stress disorder, wrote, "Suppressing the feelings only makes it harder to let them go. Expression is the opposite of depression."[7] Once you've acknowledged a feeling, you can start dealing with it appropriately. Maybe we feel sad because we're not living to our fullest potential. Maybe we feel angry because we failed to stand up for our values. Whatever the cause, remember that your feelings are neutral and temporary—meaning that simply feeling something isn't wrong or bad, and those feelings certainly won't last forever.

Something we hear a lot from participants in our courses is the desire to "fix" their feelings. If they're sad, they think they just need to stop feeling sad. The same goes for anger, jealousy, fear, frustration, guilt, etc. The thinking is that any positive emotion can stay, and any painful emotion needs to be pushed aside. Many of us have been through situations that have been so overwhelming that it was easier to ignore or suppress our emotions than to deal with them. But our feelings usually have a message for us. As we wrote earlier in the chapter, hard emotions like fear or loneliness can often point to the need for change. Maybe we need to address what's causing us to feel afraid or spend time with people who care about us. When we really sit with the emotion, practice patience, and continue to ask "Why?" until we get to the bottom of the feeling, we can learn the message it carries for us.

The point of this exercise isn't to "fix" our emotions but to work with them. After naming your feeling, write down what you think the feeling might be trying to tell you. What is the cause of the feeling? What do these emotions cause you to want to do (or not do)?

For me, journaling has been an invaluable part of defining and understanding my emotions and putting them in perspective. Sometimes, my initial definition of an emotion is superficial (e.g., "I am worried"), but as I dig deeper and write about it, I discover there's more. Journaling helps me get at the bigger question—the "why"—for feeling it. Getting at your "why" takes honest introspection. For me, that often involves an inner dialogue, asking myself questions, thinking through the answers, and sometimes writing them down. For example, I might start with:

"I'm feeling worried."

Then ask: "Worried about what?"

"I've got this big speech coming up, and I'm just not feeling prepared. I'm afraid I'm going to botch it."

"Why? Haven't you already written it? You've still got a week to prepare and practice."

"Yes, but I really don't know much about this audience, and I'm concerned my talk is not going to resonate."

"Okay, so what's one thing you can do right now to feel better about that?"

"Well, I could call some people who I know will be there and ask them what their objectives are and what would make my speech a good one for them."

"Great! What else?"

"I could research the organization. I could check out their website and see if I can find any current news about them so I can tailor my talk to them."

"And if you did that, what would that do for your worry? How would you feel?"

"I'd feel better because I'll be far more prepared, I'll deliver a more compelling talk, and I'll give something more valuable to my audience."

"Great. Then get to it."

When I write, I'm being completely vulnerable. I'm holding nothing back. I'm documenting the inner conversation to help define, understand, and take command of my emotions.

What I love about journaling is that I can go back and look at what I was feeling and thinking weeks, months, or years later and get perspective on how I've grown and changed. That hindsight helps me see things more clearly. Without the journal, what do I have? My short-term memory? Would I remember any of this? No. Writing it all down helps me document my life and appreciate my own experiences.

Step Three: Is the Feeling Serving Me?

When you ask yourself, "Is this feeling serving me?" remember to be flexible. Dr. Susan David, South African psychologist and author of *Emotional Agility*, says our tendency to have rigid responses with our emotions—like naming them as "good" or "bad" or telling ourselves we shouldn't feel a certain way—is unhelpful.[8] Getting attached to any emotion can keep us stuck—even positivity. If we only allow ourselves to feel positive and optimistic, we might stay in a toxic relationship or an unhealthy work environment because we aren't listening to our fear, sadness, or anger.

We might *want* to be happy all the time, but constant happiness is not healthy or possible. At the same time, those of us who have experienced depression or anxiety might recognize that sometimes we stay in this emotional state because it's what we've come to know, and we almost forget how to feel other emotions. It's okay to feel everything—*and* it's okay to let it go. "Research now shows that the radical acceptance of all of our emotions—even the messy, difficult ones—is the cornerstone to resilience, thriving, and true, authentic happiness," Dr. David said.

When you ask yourself if this emotion serves you, look at what's happening in your life. If you're feeling stubborn and resentful because your boss assigned you a task that you don't want to do, we have to admit that holding on to those feelings isn't helpful. On the other hand, if you're experiencing grief over the loss of a loved one, you may not want to feel the sadness, but grief takes time to move through.

Ask yourself: Is this feeling helping me become the person I want to be?

Step Four: How Can I Address This Emotion and Move Forward?

For most of us, our day-to-day emotional experiences are straightforward enough that we can find a way to move through them. With heavier emotions, however, we might get stuck in the emotion, which means we need to look for ways to leave that emotion behind. When we ask ourselves, "What can I do to address this emotion and move forward?" we're looking for answers that bring us the next clear step. Focusing on what needs to happen doesn't necessarily mean dismissing the emotion, especially if it's persistent or difficult. What we're trying to do here is avoid dwelling in an emotional space that isn't supportive.

You might think about your emotional journey as a road trip. As you travel from emotional state to state, speeding through some spots, meandering through others, you might get lost and end up somewhere unfamiliar, but you're still driving the car. Emotions are inherently temporary. We don't have to permanently move to the emotional places we visit. Just like we can reframe our thoughts, we can reframe our emotions.

Let's say you're preparing to give a presentation and you're nervous about standing up in front of a group of people. You feel your heart hammering just before you start your speech. If you were to describe that as nerves or stage fright, which many of us would, you wouldn't necessarily be wrong. But consider this: We could also interpret a pounding heart as a sign that your body is prepared and ready for a challenge. If we tell ourselves that that nervous energy is actually determination, we can move forward with confidence.

When you're ready to move on from the emotion, try the ninety-second pause. Harvard brain scientist Dr. Jill Bolte Taylor writes, "When a person has a reaction to something in their environment, there's a 90-second chemical process that happens in the body; after that, any remaining emotional response is just the person choosing to stay in that emotional loop. . . . This means that for 90 seconds you can watch the process happening, you can feel it happening, and then you can watch it go away."[9] Changing our environment, talking with a friend, going for a walk, journaling, spending time on our favorite hobbies, or exercising can also help us shift from an emotion we're ready to move on from.

TAKE COMMAND

Half the battle of working with our emotions is deciding to do it. In a world where we're encouraged to ignore or suppress our feelings instead of experiencing them fully, even acknowledging them can be an accomplishment. When we catch ourselves pushing away our emotions, we should choose instead to work with them—we'll find ourselves developing an inner strength to face any situation.

PRINCIPLE

Befriend your emotions.

ACTION STEPS

- **WORK WITH YOUR EMOTIONS.** Think about a negative emotion that is overwhelming or limiting you right now. What would it mean to you to break free of that emotion? How would that impact your life?
- **USE THE PROCESS.** The next time you feel an intense emotion like anger, sadness, frustration, or envy, stop and take a moment to work with it. Walk through these four questions:
  - How am I feeling?
  - What is the feeling telling me?
  - Is the feeling serving me?
  - How can I address this emotion and move forward?

- **OBSERVE YOUR EMOTIONS AS THEY ARISE.** If you have a hard emotion in the middle of a conversation or tough experience, try the ninety-second pause.
- **CHANGE YOUR STATE.** Change your environment, talk with a friend, go for a walk, spend time on a hobby, or exercise instead of dwelling on the emotion.

4

BUILD YOUR CONFIDENCE

Almost every student pilot does better work after his first solo flight than before. True, he may not have learned anything new in those ten minutes alone in the air, but he has acquired something vitally important: confidence. And how has he acquired it? By doing the thing he feared to do until he had a record of success behind him.

—Dale Carnegie

It was March 2014, and I was standing next to the sliding backstage door at Mark Ridley's Comedy Castle in Royal Oak, Michigan. In less than a minute, the emcee would say my name, the door would slide open, I would walk onstage, and my stand-up comedy debut would begin. The only problem: I was petrified. My heart raced, my stomach churned with anxiety, and all I could think of as I looked at the nearby fire exit was running away. "It's not too late to get out of here," I thought. While I had given many speeches over the years, it was quite another thing to stand before two hundred people who had been drinking and expected me to make them laugh. All I could think about was failing—being met with total silence and blank stares at my jokes, getting heckled because I was so bad, having some drunk throw beer at me. Talk about pressure.

My father had inspired me to sign up for a stand-up comedy class. He had done it in his seventies and said it was exhilarating. He also thought it could help me in my business. I was doing a lot of sales, and he said, "Everyone likes people who can make them laugh. Be more likeable, and you'll make more sales!" And while I had no desire to leave my day job for comedy, I had been feeling a bit complacent in my life. I wanted to challenge myself to get outside of my comfort zone, which I thought would be healthy for me emotionally. I decided it would either be stand-up comedy or jumping out of an airplane. At that moment, I wished I had picked the plane.

Then I heard the emcee's booming voice fill the building: "Please put your hands together for our next comedian, Joe Hart!" I opened the door, walked out, grabbed the mic, and went into my six-minute set, most of which was about my family. "I have six children. Four daughters who are fifteen, fourteen, twelve, and ten, and twin boys who are eight . . . and eight . . ." Yes, it was a horribly corny opener, but to my great gratitude, a few people chuckled. As I got more comfortable, better jokes and bigger laughs followed. Overall, it went pretty well. All of the things I had dreaded never happened. In fact, it was the opposite. It was actually fun. And exhilarating. The adrenaline and confidence I experienced were extraordinary.

The more I did stand-up after that night, the more confident I became, even though it didn't always go well. Sometimes I bombed horribly. I might tell the exact same joke the same way for two shows on the same night; one audience would laugh, and the other would give me a humbling silence. Twice I faced hecklers, and once I got pulled offstage for exceeding my time limit at an open mic. In all of this, even the worst situations were not as bad as I had imagined they might be. Over time, I improved my ability to read an audience and interact with them; to be less scripted, more natural, and present in the moment; to time my jokes for longer laughs (one comedian even taught me about LPM—laughs per minute—a metric I'd had no idea existed). I discovered that the tougher audiences sharpened my skills far more than the easier ones, and that a "bad" night led to more "good" ones. All of this expanded my comfort zone, and that confidence carried over to every other aspect of my life.

To take command of our lives, we must first take command of ourselves. To do that, we need confidence. Real, authentic, honest confidence—not arrogance—is the rocket fuel that can propel us through adversity. It can help us interact with others in a healthy way, take risks, and seize opportunity. Self-confidence is one of the most important parts of living a fulfilled life. The opposite—living in fear, doubt, insecurity, and worry—can destroy us.

So how can we build our self-confidence? What must we do to go from where we are to where we want to be? Two things stand out: self-efficacy and self-worth.

Self-Efficacy

Self-efficacy is our belief that we are capable of doing something. It relates directly to our ability to achieve a goal we set for ourselves. People with a high degree of self-efficacy see difficulties as challenges, not threats, because they believe they are capable, and they trust themselves to get the job done, no matter what it is. Even if they don't achieve their goal, they know they will grow and become better.

When we doubt ourselves, we might avoid tasks we view as too difficult and dwell on our failures and negative outcomes. A healthy sense of our own capability helps us see challenges as tasks to be mastered, form stronger commitments to our interests, and quickly recover from disappointing experiences. So how do we build self-efficacy? Even if we feel we don't have it now, we can grow it through taking risks, celebrating small wins, and imitating the actions of inspiring people around us.

Take Risks

First, we can build our sense of self-efficacy by taking risks. I took a risk when I stepped onto that stage—and with the very first small laugh, I started to believe that I could do it. The challenge is that the very thing you don't want to do—the thing that scares you—is the same thing that will help you build your confidence. When you do something you don't think you can do, it strengthens that muscle.

The trouble is in figuring out what constitutes a risk. For me, it felt like a real risk to start training for a marathon or do stand-up comedy. For someone else, these might not have been challenges. Everyone views risk differently based on their upbringing, abilities, past experiences, or physical makeup. A young child might think that going down the big slide at the playground is a major risk, while an older child heads down it face-first with no hesitation. Some people are scared of spontaneity; others are scared of structure. An experienced rock climber might feel there is little risk in scaling a cliff, while I would be standing on the ground wondering what I'd gotten myself into. However you view risk, building self-efficacy and confidence often means acting even when you're unsure about the outcome.

Sometimes building self-confidence looks like going against your family's beliefs to pursue personal development. Tara Westover grew up on a mountain in rural Idaho. Her parents were survivalists and paranoid about government interference in their life, which deeply affected the way she was brought up. Tara and her siblings weren't allowed to go to school, get birth certificates, or receive medical treatment. Any attempt to go against her parents' wishes resulted in verbal and physical abuse—every attempt to do something that violated their rules felt like a giant risk with incredibly intense consequences. "My life was narrated for me by others. Their voices were forceful, emphatic, absolute. It had never occurred to me that my voice might be as strong as theirs," Tara wrote in her best-selling memoir, *Educated*.

Tara's father believed that a woman's primary goal should be to get married and raise children. He made her dress in baggy clothes that wouldn't show off her figure and forced her to work in his scrapyard instead of study. With the help of some old textbooks in the basement, she managed to secretly teach herself to read and then to do algebra. Eventually she learned enough to take the ACT. Tara knew that if she could get into college, she would be able to leave home for good. It was difficult and terrifying. "The skill I was learning was a crucial one," she said, "the patience to read things I could not yet understand."

By working hard and going against the grain of her family, she managed to get a scholarship to Brigham Young University and escape her childhood home. She eventually received a scholarship to Cambridge University, where she earned a PhD in history. With each risk she took, Tara's self-efficacy grew stronger. Even though her family didn't believe in her, she learned to trust in her own capabilities and take small steps to change her situation.[1]

When I had author Keith Ferrazzi on my podcast, we talked about the relationship between fear and self-confidence. He said, "Every insecurity and fear is overcome by practicing. There's actually a psychological term called 'effective forecasting mortality salience,' which is a fancy way of saying, 'I can't possibly do that. I would die.' Well, you won't die. And the only way you'll realize you won't die is by trying it and realizing it's not so bad. The only way to figure that out is to go. It's all about practice."

Create and Celebrate Small Wins

After we begin to practice taking risks, we need to create a few small wins. If you're facing a daunting challenge that has shaken your belief in yourself, think about how you eat an elephant—one bite at a time, and with each bite will come a growing sense that you can do it. If you've been struggling to learn a new skill, you could break down each step into something that is more easily accomplished. Let's say you want to learn a new language. It takes a lot of time—sometimes years—to become fluent, so the goal can seem daunting. But if you break it down and decide that you'd like to learn two hundred of the most used words in the language first, you've got a far more achievable target. This is something you can do in a matter of weeks. Breaking down anything that feels scary or difficult into smaller goals makes the thing far more approachable.

Next, we should acknowledge and celebrate our successes when we achieve them. Think about times in your past that you have mastered something that was hard or when you succeeded at something that you didn't think was possible. How did you feel when you succeeded? Too often, we gloss over the moment and move on to the next goal. We must take the time to celebrate our small wins in a meaningful way. For some of us, that might mean going out for a special dinner with friends. For others, it might be taking a day off to do something we love.

Also, think about how you achieved that small win. What did you do to get there? Don't focus on the actual activity but on how you approached it, the way you coached yourself through it. Having a clear retrospective view of how you accomplished your win will help you do it again in the future.

Look at Your Role Models

Think about modeling those who have a strong sense of belief in themselves. When we see others act with confidence, we learn and increase our own belief that we can do it, too. One way to make this more impactful is to model someone who is similar to yourself. The more alike you are in experience, the more likely it is that your belief in yourself will grow. It also helps to seek the support of the people we look up to, especially those who know and love us. Ask them to tell you why they believe you can do it.

Finally, remember to use positive reinforcement. Remember the affirmations we created back in Chapter 1, "Choose Your Thoughts"? Creating an affirmation that reminds you that you're totally capable of doing the hard thing you've set out to do is a powerful exercise.

Self-Worth

Another way to build our confidence is by focusing on our self-worth. Self-efficacy and self-worth might seem like the same thing, but they have important differences. While self-efficacy is your belief in your ability to act and achieve, self-worth is your sense of being good enough and worthy of love. Self-efficacy is about what you can do; self-worth is about who you are. Self-worth is often confused with confidence or self-esteem, but the latter two terms often rely on things that lie outside of us, like successes and failures. Our self-worth comes solely from within. The dictionary describes it as "a feeling that you are a good person who deserves to be treated with respect."

We might have low self-worth because of how we were treated growing up, painful or discouraging life events, or even through personality traits (perfectionism, social anxiety, people-pleasing, etc.). Whatever the root cause, low self-worth is the intrinsic belief that you simply are not good enough. While our confidence and our sense of self-efficacy might change over time as we experience new challenges and roles in our lives, our self-worth—we hope—stays constant and stable, because we are all inherently worthy of respect and kindness.

Though we hope our sense of self-worth is stable, it's hard to keep it that way in a world that is flooded with negative messages. With the overbearing influence of social media, many of us have had the experience of seeing someone's harsh or critical comment on a post and instantly taking it to heart—letting it mean something about who we are as a person. There are a lot of mean people out there. The internet makes it easier for people to be horrible to one another, but we don't have to allow it to affect our self-worth.

At the age of two, Anmol Rodriguez and her mother were attacked by her father, who was angry that his wife hadn't given him a son.[2] He threw acid on them in a burst of rage. Anmol's mother died of her wounds, and Anmol's face and body were permanently scarred. Her father was arrested, and Anmol's extended family abandoned her. She spent the rest of her youth in a Mumbai-based orphanage, where she had friends and felt safe and cared for.

Her childhood was mostly happy, but when she went to college, other students whispered about her and gave her strange looks. After graduating, she landed a job as a software developer but was fired two months later. The reason? Well, she wasn't given one. She found out later from her coworkers that her face had caused some of them to feel uncomfortable.

For many people, this might have been an invitation to hide from the world. But for Anmol, the mean-spirited behavior she witnessed led to a fundamental change within. She didn't want to be a victim of other people's opinions. She felt an innate sense of self-worth that was unshakable, and she wanted to take control of her own circumstances. So, in 2016, she decided to start sharing her story on social media.

At first, her friends warned her against it. They thought she would get bullied and harassed. "I was the first acid attack survivor to share photos on social media," she said. Instead of getting flooded with hateful comments, Anmol's posts were shared and got an overwhelmingly positive response.

Anmol generally posts raw content because she wants people to see the unfiltered and unrefined version of herself. "It's not like I don't get flak for it. People do troll me and post negative comments. But I'm always mindful of the fact that it's a virtual space, so I never take anything to heart," Anmol said. Anmol is now a social media influencer and the creator of a foundation to support acid attack survivors called Sahas Foundation. She has walked in fashion shows around the world, spoken at TEDx, and acted in a short film, which earned her the "Best

Performance Female" award at the Casttree Film Festival in 2018. Comments, criticism, and judgment don't shake her innate sense of self-worth. Nothing changes the fundamental way she sees herself.

Traits of self-worth are subtle and internal. Researchers believe a strong sense of self-worth tends to arise from compassion for ourselves.[3] It's not based on achievements or conditions, like getting that promotion or checking everything off your to-do list. It's closely linked with emotional stability (which is why it's so important for us to work with our thoughts and emotions!). It doesn't shift just because we fail or make a mistake. And it doesn't rely on comparing ourselves to others and coming out on top.

To practice building self-worth:

- **BE KIND TO YOURSELF.** Speak to yourself the way you'd talk to your best friend. Return to your affirmations and your healthy routine to continue caring for your mind and body.
- **LOOK WITHIN FOR APPROVAL.** Avoid looking for external validation to feel good about who you are as a person. While it's great to build self-efficacy through external wins, self-worth can only come from within.
- **PUT SOME DISTANCE BETWEEN WHO YOU ARE AND WHAT YOU DO.** Too many of us base our self-worth on our work, our identity, or social standing. Strong self-worth is not about external achievements but about your innate worthiness.
- **DON'T COMPARE YOURSELF WITH OTHERS.** The "comparison trap" is one of the most toxic things we can fall into, particularly online. Comparison can lead us into a spiral of negative thoughts that can distract us from our purpose in life. Comparing ourselves to others, online or not, is never healthy. Avoid the comparison trap at all costs!

Self-Confidence

When we combine our self-worth and our self-efficacy, we can start to build a sense of confidence—the feeling or belief that we can rely on ourselves. Having a strong sense of confidence is similar to the strong belief you have about a friend, family member, or coworker. You know that they have inherent self-worth, and you see the good in them, no matter what they do. With this self-assertiveness, you feel like you've always got your own back—no matter what happens.

When marketing expert Portia Mount was on an expatriate assignment in Shanghai, China, she experienced extreme imposter syndrome and told herself she wasn't good enough—she doubted her abilities and felt like a fraud for being there. It was a moment of doubt in both her self-efficacy and self-worth. It had taken a lot of confidence to get to where she was, but her new role was shaking that confidence. She was one of only two Americans working at the PR firm, and she felt completely unprepared to work in such a new environment. Her clients were generally happy, but she was convinced that she wasn't doing a good job and that she wouldn't be able to keep up with the high-speed pace of corporate Shanghai. "It was a combination of overwhelm from culture shock plus worry that I would fail in this assignment I had worked so hard to achieve. I call myself a recovering overachiever. Looking back, I had put a ton of unnecessary pressure on myself to succeed," Portia said.

Late one night, Portia's phone rang—it was the CEO. "I thought, 'What is he doing calling me at ten o'clock at night?' The CEO said, 'Hey, Portia. It's Chris. I just wanted to see how you were doing. I heard you were doing good things, and I just want to let you know that if you need any help, you call me.'" Portia said, "I remember thinking, 'Why on earth would the CEO call me? Does he have spies sent out to watch me so that he can fire me?' That is what self-doubt will do—make you second-guess your competency and qualifications even though, objectively, you're 100 percent qualified." After that call, Portia took some time to reflect on what the CEO had said, and she realized that she had his support. He not only wanted her to succeed but believed she could. "I just needed to turn down the fear in my brain, accept what I didn't know, ask for help, and let go of the idea of perfection."

Portia didn't overcome her doubt overnight, but over time she got used to living in China and felt comfortable asking for help. She got encouragement from friends back in New York, and she built supportive relationships with her new colleagues in Shanghai. Her confidence in her abilities started to grow. She had good experiences with her clients, and she started speaking kindly to herself. "I cut myself a break. I was living a world away in a brand-new city where I didn't speak the language. No one expected me to have all the answers in this new work environment."

She had been telling herself, "I'm a phony. Everyone is going to find out what a phony I am as soon as I open my mouth." She had to rewrite how she spoke to herself. "The reality is, companies don't make huge investments to send people overseas who are not competent—that doesn't happen," she said. She made a point to talk herself up. When she's struggling with her confidence, she looks at her previous accomplishments to remind herself of what she's done. "I can sit down and look at my LinkedIn profile and say to myself, 'Look at your last three reviews. What do you see here? The data says that you are exactly who you are, you deserve to be here, and you are competent.'"

Portia was using positive self-talk to help build her confidence. Here's something we can do right now to turn things around: do not say something to yourself that you wouldn't say to someone you love and respect. Pick someone in your life right now. Think of someone to whom you'd never say a mean word. Pretend that person made a mistake that affected you. What would you say? More than likely, you would *not* say, "You're an idiot," or "You're a loser." Too many of us feel free to talk to ourselves that way. Instead, talk to yourself the way you would talk to the person you're imagining. You'd probably say something like "I know you made a mistake, and we all make mistakes. Let's talk about how we can fix it." By deciding to curb negative self-talk, we can create an environment for ourselves where it's okay to try new things, take chances, and make mistakes.

When you begin to doubt yourself, turn to your strengths. For example, if you're worried about an assignment, and you fear you don't know enough to complete it, focus on what you *do* know. If you're facing what appears to be a major challenge, think about the reasons your solution might work. If you're feeling down about life, shift your thinking to the things for which you are grateful right now. By talking about solutions to our problems, we emphasize positive thoughts instead of indulging in negative ones

If you decide there actually is a knowledge or experience gap you need to address, you can take quick action to do so. Michael experienced imposter syndrome as a young branch manager (we talked about his tumultuous experience in Chapter 2, "Condition Your Mind for Success"). Because he was only twenty-five, he didn't think he was worthy of holding his position, and he worried he might be exposed as incompetent to his colleagues. "I was young, and I didn't feel I knew a lot, so I realized I had two choices," Michael said. "I could continue feeling awful about myself, or I could do something. I said to myself, 'If my problem is a lack of knowledge, I can fix that by learning as much as I can.' I asked salespeople if I could join them on calls. They all said yes. I dropped into classes our trainers were teaching so I could listen. In both of these situations—sales calls and training programs—I asked the salespeople and trainers lots of questions about what they were doing and why. They were terrific—and I squeezed years' worth of learning into six months. The more I learned, the more my confidence grew, and pretty soon, I really did know what I was doing. Before I knew it, the imposter syndrome was gone."

Confidence comes from believing in yourself and in the unique abilities you have. For that reason, comparison can kill our confidence. We can't be anyone other than ourselves, and we can choose to be the best version of ourselves we can be.

When Victor Rojas was a play-by-play announcer for the Texas Rangers, he wanted to be just like the top announcer at the time, Eric Nadel. Eric was a legendary Hall of Fame announcer, and Victor did his best to imitate him. Midway through the baseball season, Victor was talking to his wife, and she said to him, "You've spent your whole time with the Rangers trying to be Eric Nadel. You've got to be yourself." Her words made Victor realize, "I can't be the second-best Eric Nadel. I have to be the best Victor Rojas."

By letting go of who he thought he should be and embracing who he was, Victor was able to spend a decade announcing for the Los Angeles Angels. Victor accepted his unique voice, and that freedom carried him through and made him more successful than he'd ever thought possible. He became legendary in his own right.

TAKE COMMAND

Self-confidence isn't something we achieve permanently. We will all go through periods of time where we feel a lack of confidence, even after years of experience. When those moments arrive, especially after failure or hardship, we have to re-center and rebuild our self-efficacy and self-worth. It's a constant continuum, where the peak is a feeling of self-confidence—a feeling of being prepared to face whatever comes your way.

Building self-confidence takes time, energy, and practice, but it is possible if we remember to adopt a growth mindset regarding self-confidence. We develop faith in ourselves—or lack thereof—based on our beliefs about our abilities, who we are, and our previous failures and accomplishments. After working with our thoughts and emotions, building self-confidence is one of the most important things we can do to take command of our lives.

PRINCIPLE

Recognize and appreciate your inherent greatness.

ACTION STEPS

- **BUILD SELF-EFFICACY.**
  - Take risks. What small chances can you take to help you feel confident outside of your comfort zone?

- Create a few small wins for yourself. Practice at first doing things that are within your reach, so you can feel a sense of accomplishment.
- Celebrate your successes. Take a moment at the end of each day to celebrate the things you got done.

- **PRACTICE SELF-WORTH.**
    - Be kind to yourself.
    - Look within for approval.
    - Separate who you are from what you do—your worth is not based on your job or your title.
    - Don't compare yourself with others.
    - Talk to yourself like you would a loved one.
- **BUILD SELF-CONFIDENCE.**
    - Talk yourself up.
    - Model those who have a strong sense of belief in themselves.
    - Use positive reinforcement.
    - Seek out the support and positive feedback of people who know and love you.

5

EMBRACE CHANGE

A man is not hurt so much by what happens, as by his opinion of what happens.

—Dale Carnegie

Luke Maguire Armstrong felt the sound of the gong's notes vibrating through the air as much as he heard it. It was 3 a.m., and the gong signaled that it was time for morning meditation. He followed the robed, silent monks as they moved from their rooms to the temple. He thought, for what felt like the millionth time, about how his trip to Asia was not supposed to lead him to a Theravada Buddhist monastery in Thailand, the name of which loosely translated to "The Temple of No Worries."

He was supposed to travel from Bangkok to Nepal to promote his recently released book, but the sudden onset of severe neck pain changed his plans. Multiple visits to doctors and chiropractors brought no answers, and he could find nothing that relieved the pain. A series of synchronicities led him to the monastery, where he thought that a week of meditation and "no worries" would help him feel better. But that was only the beginning of his experience.

Through quiet reflection at the monastery, Luke looked deep within. One day during meditation, he realized it wasn't just the physical pain that he was dealing with. He was struggling even more with the emotions his sudden pain was causing him. "I uncovered the depths of my feelings—the anxiety, the fear, the disappointment, and betrayal I felt at my body—that I hadn't known were there."

Luke had worked hard to make it as a writer. He had written a book and kept up a blog, all while performing the myriad of tasks it takes to make it as a solo writer. Now he couldn't sit at a computer for more than a few minutes without feeling severe pain. It felt like everything he had worked for was slowly being destroyed because the pain was taking over his life. "I realized that these feelings I was struggling with were telling me that I had not accepted the change in my plans and that I felt a sense of failure," he said.

This was Luke's rock-bottom moment, but at least he was developing an awareness of what had led him there.

Author and Holocaust survivor Victor Frankl wrote, "When we are no longer able to change a situation, we are challenged to change ourselves."[1] Luke couldn't do much about his circumstances, so he had to change the way he viewed them. Luke first surrendered to reality. He had been attached to the way he wanted his trip to go, and that was causing him almost as much pain as his injured neck. "When you let go of how you want life to be, you re-enter reality and start from where you are now," he said. Luke created a routine in which he practiced yoga and meditation daily, which helped him cultivate a hopeful mindset about the changes in his life. He adopted the Buddhist concept of "noble silence" by not speaking or engaging—in person or online—between 10 p.m. and 8 a.m. He cut down on the number of things he was trying to do and focused on doing a few things very well. He took more personal retreats, so he had more time for reflection. All of these practices helped him keep an open mind about his changing life plan and be confident that he would do his best, no matter what life put in front of him.

His acceptance of change has paid off. In the last four years, Luke has founded an artist and yogic retreat center called Karuna Atitlan in Guatemala, written four books, helped many other writers get published, released six music albums, and fundraised $100,000 for eighty-five Guatemalan students. Because of his ability to adapt, he completely reimagined his future in a way that deeply serves himself and others.

We've spent the last four chapters learning how to pay attention to our thoughts, work with our emotions, condition ourselves for success, and build our confidence. All those steps make us stronger, but when we experience a change, it can feel like we've been kicked off course. Change can derail our plans and discourage any of us.

Our goal in this chapter is for you to embrace change and to seek opportunities in that change.

Angela Duckworth, academic and best-selling author of *Grit: The Power of Passion and Perseverance*, said, "When you have repeated negative events in your life that are beyond your control, you learn that you are relatively helpless in the face of adversity. By contrast, a resilient response would be one where you are hunting for that small sliver that you *can* control—not the illusion you can control everything, but a resilient individual is always trying to think, 'This didn't work. This didn't work. That didn't work. But I haven't tried *this* yet.'"[2]

Whether we expect the change or not doesn't decrease the potential for frustration or resistance. It's normal to feel panicked or highly emotional when you experience sudden change. Our emotional response often correlates to our expectations. Our ability to be agile, according to Dr. Susan David, whom we introduced in Chapter 3, "Work with Your Emotions," is a skill that allows us to "navigate life's twists and turns with self-acceptance, clear-sightedness, and an open mind."[3]

The next time you are faced with change, try this:

1. Acknowledge your feelings of resistance.
2. Cooperate with the inevitable (accept what you can't change).
3. Do what you can.

Being able to surf on the waves of chaos and accept change doesn't mean that we roll over and accept every bad experience without a fight. We don't. Dr. David wrote, "Acceptance is a prerequisite for change. This means giving permission for the world to be as it is, because it's only when we stop trying to control the universe that we make peace with it. . . . And once the war is over, change can begin."

Acknowledge Your Feelings of Resistance

As a student at a religious university, Faith Smith-Place did not expect to be pregnant before she graduated. But there she was, in the fall of 2019, undeniably pregnant. She felt like she had so many factors stacked against her: she hadn't yet graduated college, she lived in the dorms, she wasn't married to the father of her child, and she had no health insurance. This wasn't how she had imagined her senior year of college—or her life.

It seemed like a challenge she might not be able to meet. And worse yet, this had long-term consequences: If she couldn't graduate college, what would that mean for her career? And if her pregnancy impacted her chances at getting a job, how could she care for her child? "I had a plan for my life. And when I got pregnant, it felt like that plan had been ripped out from under me like a rug," Faith said.

Faith felt overwhelmed, angry, and worried about her future. At first, she felt strong resistance to her new reality. But in the midst of all of the stress and morning sickness, she realized she had a choice—she could focus on the things that didn't seem to be "right," or she could focus on what was going well in her life. She was also aware of another feeling—a sense of sweetness. There was sweetness when her best friend, the father of her child, reassured her that he wasn't going anywhere—there was no one he would rather stand beside and create a family with. She felt sweetness when her father held her silently in his arms after she shared her news, and her mother said, "We don't have much, but what we have is yours," And she felt sweetness when she felt her child move for the first time. Faith said, "There came a point when I realized that I couldn't change my situation, but I could choose to see the good in it."

She also realized she had to change her approach to what she was trying to accomplish before the baby came. Shortly before final exams, the COVID-19 pandemic led her university to shut down. What was a huge obstacle for many students became a boon for her. She spent the last two weeks of her pregnancy in isolation, finishing assignments, taking exams online, and preparing her final presentations. After her last virtual shift as a writing tutor, she went into labor. Ten days after she brought her baby home, she completed her degree.

"Today, I have my dream job that I can do from the comfort of my home. I spend my days with my son and my husband, the two people I love most in the world. There's a lot of things that you can't control, but if you focus on things that bring you joy, that can get you through pretty much any situation. And sometimes those painful things turn into really beautiful things. Let them."

Faith could have given in to her initial resistance to the events in her life. She could have clung to the idea of "how it should be," but she chose not to. In response to drastic life changes, she changed her outlook and her approach to the situation.

Often, it is our resistance to change that creates that "war" within. Luke spent weeks fighting the reality of his situation until he accepted it and moved on. Faith acknowledged her resistance, then decided to accept the changes in her life—and then she did what she could to make her transition smoother. They were both experiencing great challenges, but which one do you think had the easier time? Once we stop opposing, we can create a plan and take command of what happens next.

Cooperate with the Inevitable

While I was writing this book, I flew to California to give a live keynote speech for a major, statewide conference. This was my first in-person speech since the pandemic began, and I wanted to make sure everything went right. The day before, I went to the event space and met with the organizers to review the logistics. I tested the small lavalier microphone that clipped onto my tie—I like to use my hands while I talk, and holding a microphone makes that difficult. Standing on the stage, I was happy to see that they had a ten-foot-by-ten-foot monitor hanging from the ceiling, so that I could look up and see my slides without having to turn around to see them on the large screens behind me or the small one on the floor in front of the stage. Everything seemed to be perfect, and the organizers assured me everything would go smoothly.

The next morning, it was time for my speech. I stood backstage behind a floor-to-ceiling curtain that extended from one side of the stage to the other, separating me from the audience. As the emcee introduced me, I quickly hopped up the stairs to the stage—and tripped, landing hard on my hands and knees. It wasn't painful, and the audience did not see it because I was still behind the curtain, but I wondered if they had all heard the loud "thud" I made when I hit the stage floor. I stood up, brushed myself off, and hurried out onstage—broad smile and all—ready to take that wipeout in stride. "Never let them see you sweat," I thought to myself. And then I began: "You, as leaders, are more important to your organizations than ever before." As soon I spoke, I realized that my lavalier mic wasn't working. I waited a moment and tried again. "You, as leaders, are more important to your organizations than ever before!" I said even more emphatically than the first time. The audience looked at me and one another. "We can't hear you!" someone from the audience shouted. After an awkward minute of me standing on stage and the AV team trying to make my mic work, all while the audience waited patiently, the organizer finally walked out onstage and handed me a bulky handheld mic—the very one I hated the most, the one they told me I wouldn't have to use because I'd have the lavalier mic I wanted. I remembered the process I had gone through to become a Dale Carnegie trainer and about the value of being flexible in the moment, so I started my speech like nothing had happened. Then, when I looked up, I saw that the ceiling monitor—which had been there only twelve hours earlier—was gone. "You've got to be kidding me," I thought. All of the preparation from the day before had been for nothing.

So there I was, onstage in front of a large audience, my first in-person speech in two years, feeling frustrated, disappointed, and angry. "Well, this is going to make a great story someday," I said to myself. "Time to nail this speech."

One of my favorite Dale Carnegie principles is "Cooperate with the inevitable." We have to learn how to accept what we can't change and then change the way we approach the situation. I accepted the inevitable and chose to keep right on going and give it my best. In the end, the speech went well. When I stepped off the stage, the audio engineer apologized profusely. I looked at him and said, "Do you know what, Tom? If my mic not working is the worst thing that happens to me today, it's a pretty good day."

While this story is a small example of things not going the way we want them to, it illustrates that we have to be flexible. The best way to handle something like this is to roll with it and keep going.

Do What You Can

Not all change comes in big swoops. Not all change is forced on us. And life is not made up solely of make-or-break moments that come to define who we are. Sometimes we're faced with mundane moments that require a willingness to change, even in the face of tradition.

John and Betty Mobbs manage a farm in Hauser, Idaho, using re-generative agriculture practices—they don't use herbicides, pesticides, or fertilizers, all their animals are born on the ranch, and they let nature nurture their land. John's grandparents and parents established the farm in 1972, and they taught John everything they knew. But as conventional farming became standard practice in the United States, John and Betty didn't stop to evaluate the new methods that used synthetic chemicals to maintain the fields.

When John and Betty attended a regenerative agriculture conference in 2018, they learned that synthetics (fertilizers, chemicals, and herbicides) were killing the microbes and insects that promoted soil health. John came to realize that the farming practices from the early twentieth century were still the best for the planet, because his grandparents did not use chemicals—they used chicken manure. It was also strongly suggested at this conference that they change their calving season to match nature. They had always started their calving season in February because that was how John's family taught him to do it, so that's the way it had always been done. When discussing this with another regenerative rancher, he said to John and Betty, "But it's winter— the temperature drops down to zero. Then the mud season starts. Why not start the calving season when the grass comes in, just like nature?"

"We had to take that information and say, 'Well, wait a minute here. My grandfather and father ranched this way. Do we want to continue that, or should we break that tradition?'" John said. They had never considered that there might be a better way to do things. They wanted to respect John's grandfather's and father's wisdom, which made them feel resistant to change, but as they learned more about ecology agriculture, they concluded that they were shortchanging their livestock and the health of their farmland. Instead of taking an "all or nothing" approach, John and Betty found that they could hold to their family values by embracing ecological agriculture and adopting regenerative practices, while also admitting that some methods (like starting the calving season in February) didn't make sense for them anymore.

Together, they decided to do the hard work of changing the way they farmed. Betty said, "Our number one value is we are stewards of the land, the animals, and our customers. We treat people how we want to be treated." By embracing change, John and Betty have made their part of the world a healthier and happier place.

Part of accepting change is understanding that sometimes, we'll have to make a choice—continue doing what's comfortable or change and accept a new way of life, one that might be better for us and for those around us. Change won't always come to you. Sometimes you'll have to go out and meet it head-on.

But you know, there's also a way that change can become an unhealthy habit. Yuri Kruman thought he was good at handling change. When he was nine, he had immigrated from Russia to the United States and learned a new language and culture. He married a French engineer, left the field of neuroscience to go to law school, and felt confident he could take life's changes in stride. His life seemed to be defined by change—in a good way. But as a young adult, the constant changes threw him for a loop. He graduated from law school in 2009 in the middle of the financial crisis—with $250,000 in student debt. There were very few jobs, so he had to take a job in finance to pay the bills—not the kind of career he had expected to have. He hated finance, so he went from one job to another in health care, consulting, startups, product management, and human resources, and never felt satisfied.

When his two-month-old daughter was diagnosed with cancer, Yuri's life came to a screeching halt. "I just stopped and thought to myself, 'What am I doing? I've been grinding myself to dust. My marriage is not doing well. My kid is sick with cancer. I need to stop just reacting to things that change and start being proactive about them. I need to cut away the fat and focus on what matters.'"

Yuri realized that he thought he was "good" at change, but in truth, he was using constant change to drive his life instead of slowing down long enough to think about what he wanted and what his family needed. Yuri hadn't been making his choices consciously—change had become a reaction to discomfort. He decided to take command and choose what he wanted in life, instead of using change as a crutch.

At the time, his family lived in New York, and they decided to prioritize their health and safety by moving to Israel, where he felt it would be safer, more affordable, and more relaxed. "I knew change was coming, so we thought, 'Why not just lean in and go for it? Let's do something about it instead of waiting for it to come to us,'" Yuri said. He stopped job hopping and started doing what he loved and was good at—telling stories and empowering people. His book *Be Your Own Commander in Chief* shares his newfound understanding about living a meaningful life in a chaotic world.

Today, Yuri is the CEO of HR, Talent & Systems, an award-winning chief people officer, and a top-rated leadership coach. He drew from his experiences—and the wisdom he gained from them—and built a platform to deliver corporate learning and development programs for *Fortune* 500 companies and tech startups, and help millennials and Gen Zers find their direction in life.

"Your goal in life shouldn't be to win prizes, but to find truth. And I'm learning that looking for truth means not just embracing change but also driving it in a thoughtful way. Figure out who you are and what you're good at, and drive the change in your life toward that focus," Yuri said. He soon learned that if you're serious about embracing change, you will have to embrace failure, too. "But failure is just iteration," Yuri said. Sometimes we can perceive a change in our lives as a failure—getting laid off, a relationship ending, losing out on an opportunity. But as Yuri said, "Take the surprises and disappointments and unplanned incidents of your life and use them to direct your life toward where you want to go." Embrace those changes. Drive those changes forward toward something new. And seek truth and growth in the process.

TAKE COMMAND

At the heart of all of these stories is the experience of moving through resistance, embracing change, and experiencing joy and meaning despite hardship. While we can all struggle with change, it doesn't have to be painful. In fact, if we approach changes in our lives with intention and awareness, we may find an opportunity for growth that we didn't expect. One might even say that the most important moments of our lives are the hardest, and the way we triumph is to create meaning that helps us move forward. To do that, we must keep an open mind and be willing to meet what's coming.

PRINCIPLE
Find opportunity in change.

ACTION STEPS

Think about a situation you're facing right now that requires change—either externally or internally. Do the following exercise:

- **ACKNOWLEDGE YOUR FEELINGS OF RESISTANCE.** It's your resistance to change that makes it that much harder. How are you resisting the change that's needed? How does that show up—in your mindset, thoughts, feelings, or actions?

- **COOPERATE WITH THE INEVITABLE (ACCEPT WHAT YOU CAN'T CHANGE).** Think about what is inevitable in this situation. What is bound to happen—no matter how much you wish it wouldn't? What are the factors that you can do nothing about? What must you accept so you can move on?
- **CHOOSE YOUR ACTIONS AND DO WHAT YOU CAN.** Once you accept the inevitable, think about what can be done. Even when you accept what's coming, there are still actions you can take to make the best of the situation. Write down what actions you can take, make a plan, and start it promptly.

6

MOVE BEYOND REGRET

This day is too precious to be corroded by acid worries and vitriolic regrets. Keep your chin high and your thoughts sparkling, a mountain brook leaping in the spring sunshine. Seize this day. It will never come again.

—Dale Carnegie

Ally Love grew up with a Black mother and a white father at a time when biracial couples weren't often accepted in American culture.

When she was a little girl, Ally knew that every holiday was split in half—she would spend the morning with her dad's parents and the afternoon with her mom's parents. Nothing struck her as particularly unusual about this until Ally was about ten years old. One Christmas, she and her family pulled up to her paternal grandparents' house. Her mom was in the driver's seat, and Ally, her sister, and her father got out of the car. They said goodbye to their mother, something they'd done every year before, on every holiday.

But on that day, it didn't sit right with Ally. "There was a pain in my heart because while my mom is driving away from her family, my grandparents are there at the door, greeting us with open arms and smiles," she said. She had never questioned the fact that they separated for the holidays. "It suddenly didn't make sense to me. My parents were together and married but didn't spend holidays together, as if we were in some type of broken home. I couldn't understand why or what this meant," she said.

Ally's mom drove away to go see her side of the family. While Ally would also see her maternal grandparents later that day, it hurt her feelings that her mom wasn't there with her. "I wasn't mad at her for not coming in. I wasn't mad at my grandparents for not asking why she didn't come in. I was just overall hurt and offended—at such a young age without the ability to understand what was going on—at the fact that my mom and my grandparents weren't able to share the holidays together," she said.

What she didn't know at the time was that her paternal grandfather didn't agree with Ally's father's decision to marry a Black woman—she was never invited into their home.

Ally's grandfather passed away while she was in college, which led to her first major life regret. "While I don't have a lot of regrets, this one hit home: I really wish I'd taken the time to question his position, to question why he believed what he believed, to gather insight and to be curious," she said. "My regret is that I wasn't curious enough to ask these questions when it felt uncomfortable for me. While I trusted my parents and grandparents, and I felt they had shown so much love to me and my sister, I never got the chance to ask, 'Why did you treat my mom the way you treated her?'" She regrets that she never got to teach her grandfather, to understand his perspective, or to share her experience of what it meant to be a biracial Black woman in the United States.

While Ally can't go back in time, her regret has shaped the way she thinks about her relationships with her living relatives and led her to be courageous about having hard conversations with family members. She's been able to speak bravely and openly about her perspective while seeking to understand her relative's viewpoints—even when she doesn't agree with them. "Our families eventually came together. My grandmother is still alive and a part of my life. We are more integrated as a family in this day and age, and we've grown together," Ally said. "I'm proud of my father and proud of my family as a collective because of the growth, the bravery, and the fact that they've all been willing to listen and get better and change and unify in leaning toward being one family."

We all make mistakes, and sometimes regret—or the feelings of guilt or shame that come with it—keeps us from moving forward. While regret, shame, and guilt are different emotions, they all play into how we deal with and move past the moments where we inevitably misstep.

We might feel regret when we've made a small mistake at work, or when we failed to act or made the wrong decision in another situation, and we don't like how things turned out. It might be minor, like regretting that you ate too much. Or you might feel regret over something major, like hurting someone you love by saying something inconsiderate or mean. There are varying shades and degrees of regret, but the core is that something you did or did not do had an impact that you wish it hadn't. Past regrets can be oppressive; they can become barriers between you and the life you want to live, eat away at your self-confidence, and keep your stress levels high. Once you resolve past regrets, it's much easier to take command of your thoughts and emotions.

Author Dan Pink conducted the World Regret Survey, which collected entries from 17,000 participants across 105 countries. After the study—which he shared in his book *The Power of Regret*—he came to think of regret as the most misunderstood and the most transformative emotion. The findings revealed that beneath the surface reason for regret—regrets about not asking that person out, or not taking a chance and starting your own business—there are what he calls core regrets. Core regrets are broken down into four categories:

FOUNDATION REGRETS: regrets that focus on building a proper foundation for life. You would have a foundation regret if you regretted not going to school or saving for retirement.

BOLDNESS REGRETS: these center around what you didn't do, like not taking a chance on starting a business, or not asking someone out that you really liked.

MORAL REGRETS: where you feel you've missed the chance to do the right thing, or when you did act, you did the wrong thing.

CONNECTION REGRETS: regrets around relationships that came apart, or where you failed to put energy into a relationship and it ended.

Pink writes, "These four regrets operate as a photographic negative of the good life. If we understand what people regret the most, we also understand what they value the most. So this negative emotion of regret gives us a sense of what makes life worth living."[1]

Regret can be far more beneficial than we might think. Although regret and the other emotions that come along with it can feel uncomfortable, and most of us would rather avoid feeling those emotions, they can signal to us that we've done something that we would like to amend or correct—or never do again. These emotions can tell us that we need to make up for what we did, apologize, or take action that moves us in the direction we want to go. Regret and guilt can act as pointers to the kind of behavior that will help us avoid feeling that way again.

Take a closer look at the core regrets above. What do you notice? When you think about them, it becomes evident that regrets around actions we didn't take outnumber regrets about actions we did take. We are far more likely to regret what we didn't do than what we did.

We need to handle regret like we do other emotions. Just like we should not suppress or ignore any emotion, we also shouldn't deny our regrets. The "no regrets" philosophy is about as useful and realistic as saying "no emotions." The question isn't whether we should feel regret, but what to do when it arises.

When you think about situations that leave you feeling a sense of guilt and regret, do the following exercise: Review the situation so you understand it fully. As you look at the matrix below, consider:

Regret Framework

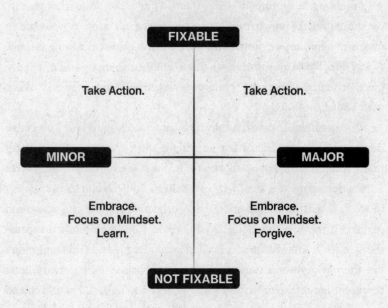

1. Is the impact of what I did or didn't do major or minor?
2. Is it fixable or not?

Michael and I have used a simple *x/y* matrix as a tool to navigate regret. On the *x* axis, from left to right, is importance. We have to ask ourselves if the topic we regret is something of major importance (right side) or minor importance (left side). We use the *y* axis to consider whether the thing we regret is fixable (top) or not fixable (bottom). Using this framework, we can consider whether something is major and fixable, minor and fixable, major and not fixable, or minor and not fixable. Where the event or circumstance falls on the matrix will guide what you do.

Once we've considered the event and where it falls on the matrix, then we must decide on the actions that can be taken and do them. There may be things we can do to repair or amend the situation, and we should waste no time in doing them. After we've done what we can, we should reflect on what we learned from the situation so we don't do it again. What can we do to make sure we don't make the same mistake twice? Finally, work through whatever emotions remain—like sadness, guilt, or shame—using the framework we outlined in Chapter 3, "Work with Your Emotions."

For example, I was on a call once with a colleague, and I was edgy during our conversation. I felt impatient, and I spoke to him in a way that I wouldn't want to be spoken to. It didn't seem to have much of an impact during the call, but I felt regret after I hung up and had a moment to think about the conversation. I went through the exercise above and realized that while the incident was minor, I could certainly do something to fix it. After reflecting, I called my colleague and said that I didn't like the way my words came out when we spoke the day before. It didn't represent me or the principles I live by, so I apologized. He told me no apology was needed, but I'm also sure he appreciated it. The incident was minor and fixable, and I was able to move on quickly from it.

On the other hand, we also face situations that are minor and not fixable, and despite their small impact, we still dwell on them. It still comes down to what is doable. Wendy Wang was fresh on her first full-time job, and she needed to lead a kickoff session via video conference with a group of outside participants. Her manager left her to prepare for it—the trust was wonderful, but Wendy didn't have a schedule or a standard operating procedure ("SOP") to work from. Even more troubling, her clients requested to use a different video conference software than Wendy had used in the past, which left her feeling even more unprepared. Wendy did her best to test the software and familiarize herself beforehand, but it didn't help. The class was a disaster—the internet kept going out, the software kept disconnecting, and her co-leader was having his own technical difficulties, too. All these distractions led her to make big mistakes during the presentation. Wendy didn't have a plan B to remedy the training session, and the participants were very disappointed. It was her first time leading a group like this, and she felt embarrassment and regret about the way it had gone.

While Wendy couldn't go back and redo the presentation, she could learn from this experience and make changes to the way she presented in the future. She took the time to develop an SOP and a schedule for the next training sessions. Then she made sure she understood how to troubleshoot any technical glitches that might arise. By the next class, she felt completely prepared. Her regret had paid off because she learned from it to improve her performance.

Regrets that are major and fixable may not always be fixable in the way we expect. Ron Carter developed the streaming technology for video doorbells that has changed the way we keep our homes safe. When I had Ron on my podcast, he told me the story of one of his biggest regrets and how he navigated the situation. "In 2003 and 2004, we were nowhere near having the ability to stream video," he said. "At that time, everything was considered closed circuit, where video content was either transmitted via an antenna or a wire." When Ron's mother had two hip surgeries and could not answer her door, Ron had the idea to connect a BlackBerry cell phone with a Panasonic video recorder so that his mom could see who was at the door and decide if she needed to answer it or not. "It took a day and a half to get the video, but it worked," Ron recalls. He spent years and his life's savings developing the streaming technology that powers many of the devices we use today. "One of the reasons I received a patent on this technology is because I was so far ahead of everyone," Ron said.

Seeing an enormous business opportunity, Ron brought in a business partner to commercialize his invention. "He was a very, very smart person, and I trusted him completely. That was my mistake. I didn't realize he was going to destroy me. Through a series of maneuvers, he took control of the business—and then he kicked me out. I was devastated," Ron says. "I trusted him, and he took everything from me. I lost my company, and I was basically broke. I didn't even see it coming." This betrayal gnawed at Ron, agonizing him for months and affecting his ability to trust other people in his life. Ron felt powerless, like he couldn't do anything and had no options.

Because Ron had lost all of his savings, he took a job as a UPS driver to make ends meet. It was then that he discovered e-commerce was booming . . . as was the theft of products delivered to people's front doors. "When I did the research, I realized that e-commerce was a five-trillion-dollar industry, so I had the idea of developing an AI-based drone security product that could protect home deliveries and stop thieves." After years of development, Ron now holds a patent on a new technology that is launching shortly and is poised to disrupt the home security industry—artificial intelligence is a significant upgrade over previous video doorbell systems. But how did Ron get over his feelings of regret from trusting his former business partner so that he could move forward? Ron says it came down to acceptance and action. "I came to believe, especially through my faith—which, as a cancer survivor, is especially important to me—that the timing for my first business wasn't right. I believed that God had better things in store for me, so I became open to receiving something better than my first company. Plus, I knew I had to let go of what had happened because it was killing me."

Can you imagine having everything taken from you, the feeling of despair you might have if you were betrayed by someone you trusted? Ron could have given in to his regret, anger, and sadness, but his beliefs and his mindset helped him work through his experience, move forward day by day, and forgive himself.

Finally, let's look at situations that are major and not fixable. Michael had regrets about the end of his mother's life. They were at a convention together when his mom, Rosemary, suddenly became very ill. She was rushed to the hospital, where they diagnosed her with uterine and ovarian cancer. Rosemary began treatment right away and went to the hospital on a weekly basis.

"It didn't feel real for a long time," Michael said. "I don't think that I could accept that it was not only real, but it was one of the worst kinds of cancer that she could get. I kept trying to come up with an easy solution to the whole issue, but there was no easy solution." At the same time, Michael was at a point in his career where he was working ninety-five-plus hours a week on average, and in the early stages of his mother's treatment, he let work take up time instead of spending it with her. Rosemary lived in New York, and Michael lived in California, so Michael only visited her once a month, for a couple of days. He was still telling himself that she would be fine.

Within four months of her diagnosis, Rosemary accepted that her cancer was terminal and decided to stop treatment. The change in direction rocked Michael, and he struggled to accept it. He was angry at the situation, and still couldn't make himself break away from work. While his mom took one last trip to Europe with some other family members, Michael continued with life as usual.

At some point, Michael shook himself out of his denial. Once he accepted that his mother's life was ending, he regretted the lost time with her. This was a major regret, and the lost time was unfixable. But he decided to take steps to be there for her with the time she had left. "I spent the last few weeks of her life with her, and it was very special. I hadn't taken that much time away from work in five years, let alone at one time," he said. "I watched her live every moment she could. She was kind and gentle with other people and perked up for every phone call or visit. She never complained. I held her hand as she passed away, and I was delighted to be there—she was an example of how to die well."

Michael could have ruminated and beaten himself up over his regrets, but this likely would have distracted him from the last few weeks of his mother's life. He accepted that he needed to focus on the present moment and ultimately forgave himself, which helped him be there for her.

Sometimes we have to surrender to our experiences. I think of the Serenity Prayer here, which has helped so many people move on from hard experiences in life that feel out of control: "God grant me the serenity to accept the things I cannot change, the courage to change the things that I can, and the wisdom to know the difference." As we said in the previous chapter, we're not suggesting you grudgingly accept what has happened. Embracing and accepting our past mistakes means that we take the lessons from them and move on. Staying stuck in regret, guilt, or shame helps no one.

This is where our perspective becomes incredibly important, and everything we've learned about dealing with thoughts and emotions comes into play. I tend to have a belief that things work out for the best. That perspective helps me move on from a hard situation, even when I deeply wish I had made another choice. Even if I can't fix the mistake, I still ask myself what I can do from here and how I can make things better.

Forgiving yourself and others can be harder than it sounds. Most of us struggle with forgiveness, both of ourselves and others. In a Dale Carnegie *Take Command* podcast interview, Marshall Goldsmith, who wrote *The Earned Life*, told me about the idea of impermanence. He likes the idea of the Buddha's teaching that "Every time I take a deep breath, I am a new me." Marshall told me that we are always starting over with every breath. We get a chance to start over with every new moment. "What's healthy about that is, number one, you're much better at forgiving yourself for previous sins when you think about them as the mistakes of a previous version of you," he said. In other words, put some distance between you and the actions you took or didn't take. They didn't make you a bad person—they just contributed to a better version of you. "And the other thing about that mindset is that it keeps you from living in the past," he said. The last thing we want is to let regret or guilt keep us from moving past the inevitable mistakes we make.

TAKE COMMAND

Learning to move on from our regrets is a skill we must develop if we're to take command of our lives. Start practicing now. While the past can't be redone, we can shape the future we want if we decide to do it.

PRINCIPLE

Confront your regrets, make amends, and move on.

ACTION STEPS

Think about a situation about which you have some regret. Write down the answers to the following prompts:

- **REVIEW THE SITUATION SO YOU UNDERSTAND IT FULLY.** What happened? Note that you should separate what actually happened—the events—from how you feel about it.
- **WORK WITH THE REGRET MATRIX.**
  - Is the impact of what I did or didn't do major or minor? Think about the impact on everyone involved. How did your actions impact the other person? How did they impact you?
  - Is it fixable or not? Is there anything at all that you can do to improve the situation—even in a small way? If not, be honest with yourself about that.

- **DECIDE ON THE ACTIONS THAT CAN BE TAKEN AND DO THEM.** There is always something to be done—an apology, a repair, or simply forgiving yourself. Decide what you can do to address the situation and do it.
- **DETERMINE WHAT YOU'VE LEARNED FROM THE SITUATION SO YOU CAN PREVENT IT FROM HAPPENING AGAIN.** After you've done the repair work, reflect on what you've learned from this situation. What can you do to make sure this doesn't happen again? How do you need to change your behaviors or mindset to reflect your new understanding?
- **FORGIVE YOURSELF AND WORK WITH THE EMOTIONS THAT COME FROM FEELING RE-GRET.** Use the emotional framework from Chapter 3, "Work with Your Emotions," to work with any lingering emotions from the experience.

7

DEAL WITH STRESS

Our fatigue is often caused not by work, but by worry, frustration and resentment.

—Dale Carnegie

"What the heck is this?" I asked my dermatologist as I pointed to the painful rash on my neck and upper left shoulder.

"I think you have shingles," she said.

"What? Shingles? How can that be? I thought shingles only affected older people, and I'm not that old."

"Well," she said, "younger people can get them, too. Have you been under a lot of stress lately?"

The question hit me hard. In the prior twelve weeks, I had traveled to Taipei, Taiwan; Rio de Janeiro, Brazil; Athens, Greece; and South Carolina, Michigan, Illinois, Washington, Oregon, North Carolina, and Missouri in the United States. Most of these trips involved meetings and presentations, some of which were high-pressure and many of which included time zone changes of one to twelve hours. Exercising consistently was nearly impossible. I was eating out for most of my meals, and I found myself relying on energy drinks to overcome gnawing fatigue in the morning and late afternoon. I had put enormous pressure on myself to give my best in all of my meetings, all while trying to be the best husband and father I could be—but if I were being honest with myself, I was absolutely depleted.

"Yes, I've been pushing myself pretty hard these past few months. And I know stress can cause heart and other physical problems, but shingles? I thought shingles were caused by a virus. How does stress cause a virus to occur?" I asked.

"Well, it is caused by a virus, but stress can weaken your immune system, which can make you more susceptible to a viral infection, or it might reactivate the virus if you've had it and it's been dormant."

This was a wake-up call. Even though I was only forty-nine (and kept reassuring myself that forty-nine was the new twenty-nine), I had to be honest about the incredible stress I had been putting on myself—not just the physical exhaustion of travel and work, but also the self-inflicted pressure to perform at a high level, the fear of making a mistake and looking bad, and the worry about what people would say. But to think that any of that emotional strain could cause a physical reaction like shingles told me I had to do a better job at handling stress—and I had to cut myself some slack. I unplugged from email, work, and other responsibilities over the holidays and resolved to pay closer attention to my stress levels moving forward and to slow down when they began to go off the charts. I've done okay, but this is an ongoing effort.

We all face stressful situations that can undermine our health, relationships, and lives. Taking command of our stress means recognizing it and acting on it before it hurts us or others. You might say, "That's easier said than done." And you're right. Sometimes our stress can feel so overwhelming that it seems almost impossible to break free. Although it can appear that way at times, the reason we did the work in the previous chapters was to create a sense of autonomy and capability, to learn how to work with ourselves and the challenges we face. Up to this point, we've worked hard to choose the right thoughts, deal with our emotions, develop our mindset and confidence, embrace change, and move on from regret. All of the tools we've gained directly relate to our ability to handle stress. Remember that we always have a choice; making good decisions about our thoughts and emotions in stressful situations is more than half the battle. That's what this chapter is about—learning to act on stress before it acts on us.

What Is Stress?

Stress is a normal human reaction. It is a response to internal events (such as a thought or memory) or external ones, also called "stressors." That stimulus can come from within or outside of us, and it can cause us to feel emotional, too. Stress can feel like a negative emotion when it's actually a physiological response. We are supposed to experience stress when we face challenges or threats. It can help us adapt to new situations and keep us motivated and alert.[1] When we feel stressed, we might feel our heart beat faster, we might breathe heavier, our palms might get sweaty, or we might struggle to think clearly. We've all felt this fight-or-flight response.

Stressors come in all shapes and sizes. Major stressors can include losing a job, moving, losing a loved one, or going through a breakup. Minor stressors can include tough conversations at work, feeling overwhelmed by our to-do list, or being late for school.

Stress vs. Anxiety

Before we go on, let's distinguish between stress and anxiety, words we often use interchangeably. Although we are constantly learning more about stress and anxiety and how they work, we know enough to distinguish between the two experiences.

We experience anxiety when we have persistent and unrealistic or exaggerated worries that don't stop, even after the stressor goes away. We feel stressed about real things that happen (like waiting on a payday to pay our bills). Anxiety is when we interpret those real things in an exaggerated way (even after we pay the bills, we still worry that we can't make ends meet and that we'll "never have enough money"). Anxiety can feel like dread or fear, even when the situation doesn't pose a real threat. Anxiety can continue after the stressful event has ended, and if it's serious enough, it can escalate into a disorder. (Just to be clear, for the rest of the chapter, we'll be talking about general stress and anxiety, not anxiety disorders, which are more severe and require medical help to deal with. An anxiety disorder would fall into the category of extreme distress, as opposed to ordinary stress.) You might feel anxiety if you often catastrophize or put too much emphasis on mistakes or things you think are "wrong."

Usually, stress is short-term. Anxiety can linger. Stress is a response to a recognized threat. Anxiety may not have an identifiable trigger.[2]

How Stress Shows Up

We all react differently to stress. I might feel stressed out about getting somewhere on time, while you may not feel the same kind of pressure. Maybe you feel stressed at the thought of giving a speech, but for someone else, it's just another thing they do. If you feel so afraid of messing up while giving the speech that it keeps you up at night and makes you feel nervous even after the event has passed, you might be feeling anxiety.

The important thing is to understand what stresses us out and find ways to deal with it before it becomes chronic. Think about a time when you experienced significant stress. How did it feel? How did your stress levels affect your life? When you think about examples, you might notice that stress is sometimes helpful. As any student who decided to get that essay done right before the deadline knows, some stress helps us get things done. Before we move on, let's understand the difference between ordinary stress and chronic stress.

Ordinary Stress

We actually need some degree of pressure to function. *Eustress*, which means "good" stress, is beneficial. We experience eustress when we are learning something new or taking on tasks that are just far enough outside of our comfort zone to challenge us but aren't so hard that we feel we can't succeed.[3]

Tim Reilly was just starting out as an attorney at a government agency and was mediating a negotiation for a case with a colleague named Rachel. They were standing outside the room where two opposing sides of a civil rights case were waiting for mediation to begin. Rachel looked at Tim and said, "Sometimes I feel nervous right before these start. What if something goes wrong, or we can't get them to see eye to eye?" Tim said, "I always get butterflies . . . but instead of feeling stressed by the butterflies, I take it as a sign that I care about what's happening." Tim reframed his emotional experience as a sign of care (instead of a sign of distress) and rose to the challenge. Recognizing what he was feeling and being able to use it constructively enabled Tim to not only avoid the negative impacts of worry but perform at a higher level. The right kind of stress can help us perform well and accomplish our goals.

Chronic Stress

Stress becomes a problem when our reactions to it cause us to remain in a state of anxiety or unease for a long time. With chronic stress, there's never relief, and it feels like the pressure doesn't let up. When we are under constant stress, our bodies and mind have no time to recover. Think about our immune systems. They need to encounter foreign bacteria and germs to stay robust. That's an example of good stress, or eustress. However, even a healthy immune system will falter under a constant attack of germs and bacteria that it isn't prepared to handle.

Our bodies are well equipped to handle small amounts of stress, but chronic, long-term stress causes severe damage to our immune system—increased heart rate and blood pressure, susceptibility to infection, risk of diabetes, hair loss, headaches, digestive issues, or even an outbreak of shingles. This is why managing our stress is so important. If we fail to do so, we can suffer long-term consequences.[4]

How to Reframe Stress

An interesting study tracked thirty thousand adults in the US over eight years. The participants were asked the following question: "How much stress have you experienced in the last year?" Participants also had to share whether they believed that the stress they experienced was harmful for their health. Over the course of the study, researchers looked at public death records to determine who died. Unfortunately, those participants who said they experienced a lot of stress the year before had a 43 percent increased risk of death. The good news, however, is that was only the case for those who *believed* that stress was harmful for their health. Those who didn't see stress as harmful had no higher likelihood of dying. Surprisingly, they had a lower risk of dying than other groups in the study—including those who reported low levels of stress. The study showed that our beliefs about stress and how it impacts us can have as much or more of an effect than the stress itself.[5]

Another study at Harvard University measured what happened when participants thought of their stress as helpful, like Tim Reilly in the story above. They were told to think of a pounding heart and fast-paced breath as simply signs of preparing for action. Those who were trained to view their stress as beneficial for their overall performance felt more confident, and less stressed and anxious.[6]

Dr. Kelly McGonigal, health psychologist and lecturer at Stanford University, says, "When you choose to view your stress response as helpful, you create the biology of courage. And when you choose to connect with others under stress, you can create resilience. . . . When you choose to view stress in this way, you're not just getting better at stress, you're actually making a pretty profound statement. You're saying that you can trust yourself to handle life's challenges."[7]

A Simple Tool for Easing Stress: The Problem-Solving Technique

When you're stressed out, how often do you feel as if you can do anything about it? Often, the way we handle a given situation causes more stress than the actual problem itself. One of the most notable parts of stress and anxiety is feeling a lack of control. If we're afraid of the outcome of a given situation, we might avoid making decisions, which makes the anxious feelings worse. If we're not sure what to do, we might spend too much time thinking about our options and not enough time acting. This creates a negative feedback loop. It's not only the stressor that causes problems but the belief that you can do nothing about it.

We discussed in previous chapters the power of our mindset, and this includes the way we think about our emotional experiences. It's totally normal to feel emotional when we're stressed out. Some of us are simply more emotional than others. But we don't want to get stuck in the emotion—the key to managing stress is knowing how to think about the problem and act, no matter what we're feeling. Even though it can seem like it in the moment, we are never powerless.

One of the great tools Dale highlighted in *How to Stop Worrying and Start Living* and that Michael and I use all the time to manage stress is the "problem-solving technique." This approach helps us get to the root cause of our stress. When you're feeling stressed, write out and answer the following questions:

1. **WHAT IS THE PROBLEM?** Really challenge yourself here because sometimes what we think is the problem isn't actually the

problem. Before accepting the first thing that pops into your mind, make sure you've gotten to the real issue.

2. **WHAT ARE THE CAUSES OF THE PROBLEM?** You might list a few things or many things, but whatever the number of "causes," do your best to summarize and rank them.

3. **WHAT ARE THE POSSIBLE SOLUTIONS?** Feel free to brainstorm this, but again, challenge yourself around the top potential solutions.

4. **WHAT IS THE BEST POSSIBLE SOLUTION?** Now it's time to focus. Pick the best solution, and then commit to at least one thing you can do, right now, to move toward that solution. Action is key because doing something is a critical part of reducing worry.

Ahmed Kamal is a good example of someone who applied that problem-solving approach to understand and act on his stress. Ahmed served on the residential board for the property where he and his family live in Alexandria, Egypt. In this role, he felt incredibly stressed. As the treasurer, Ahmed helped manage more than five hundred units—which meant hundreds of people with potential complaints like leaking pipes, loud neighbors, clogged-up toilets, and appliances that didn't work. On top of this, Ahmed also worked full-time in the sales industry. One day, after a barrage of angry messages on a WhatsApp thread the tenants used to communicate among themselves, Ahmed felt overwhelmed. The stress of being treasurer was affecting his sleep, and he had many restless nights. Without realizing it, Ahmed brought that stress into his family life. Ahmed's wife told him his stress was affecting her and their two daughters. Since he didn't want his family to bear the brunt of his emotional state, Ahmed knew he had to make changes—and he decided to start with the problem-solving technique.

First, he asked himself, "What's the problem?" That was easy for him to define: his work as the treasurer was stressing him out and clearly affecting his sleep, his health, and his family. If he didn't do something, all these things would get worse. Ahmed didn't even want to think about that.

Second, he thought about the causes of that problem. For one thing, he knew that the WhatsApp thread that everyone used to communicate was full of negativity, passive aggression, and criticism—every time he engaged with that thread, he was in a bad mood for hours. He also thought about the interactions he had with his fellow board members, whom he expected more from. He felt he was doing all the work when they should contribute more. He identified these as the two biggest causes of his stress.

Then Ahmed came up with a long list of potential solutions and ultimately identified his top three "best solutions." First, he stopped participating in the WhatsApp text thread and left the group. He committed to addressing situations with people one-on-one, but he refused to take part in an insulting and toxic group chat. Next, Ahmed decided to let go of his expectations of others and instead focus on his own workload. Finally, Ahmed decided that, while he had to honor his commitment to serve as treasurer, he would not run for the position again when his term expired. Ahmed knew he could not make everyone on the board act more civilly, but he could remove himself from the situation, and he could turn off notifications that constantly reminded him of the stressful dynamic. Ahmed took command of the situation to the best of his ability.

These actions immediately changed Ahmed's mood and outlook. He felt relaxed, especially when he was at home with his family. He also committed to being more aware of stress—to see it as soon as it appeared. Ahmed said he had to "have his sensors on" for chronic stress, so he would know when it was becoming an issue before it took over his life. He had told himself he could "handle it," and he might have handled it, but his family—his children—could not.

When we fail to listen to our body's need to slow down, we might experience burnout. Burnout is not just a state of mind or an emotional response to prolonged stress. Research shows that it can harm our personal and social functioning, overwhelm our cognitive functions, affect our hormone systems—all of which lead to changes in the way our brains work. Along with mental and emotional effects, burnout can cause insomnia, nausea, headaches, heart palpitations, shortness of breath, and panic attacks.[8]

A recent Gallup study showed that 2.7 million workers in Germany feel burnout. In the United Kingdom, a survey of human resource directors showed that almost 30 percent of respondents reported widespread burnout throughout their organizations.[9]

Negin Azimi experienced burnout in a dramatic way. Negin was born in Iran and left at the age of three. Her mother immigrated to Sweden, and though they thought life would be easier, they struggled financially for years. After attending a Dale Carnegie Course when she was fourteen, Negin learned how to speak in front of people—and she loved it. She couldn't get a job, so she started her own consulting company at the age of sixteen. She got very good at it, and the biggest companies in Sweden hired her to speak. They loved hearing a young person from a different background talk about life. She became the youngest organizer for TEDx in the world. She won awards for organizing TEDx in Sweden, and she ran it for several years. She was also a board member for the SOS Children's Villages for four years.

All of that was wonderful until Negin hit a wall. At the age of eighteen, she experienced burnout. The burnout was serious—she didn't get out of bed for two years. She stopped attending high school in her last year because she was so sick.

With so much time in bed, Negin thought about how she had arrived at this point. In hindsight, her burnout was not a total surprise. Her body had told her many times that she was stressed, tired, and didn't feel good, but she didn't listen. Negin feels that this experience was both the worst and the best thing that ever happened to her. While she had to battle illness and exhaustion, it taught her how to have a better connection with her mind and body. She was thrilled to accomplish everything she wanted, but she also learned that none of it mattered if she didn't have her health. Negin's greatest lesson was that "everything is like water—everything changes all the time, and you have to go with the flow and listen to your body and soul." Negin slowly regained her strength and worked her way back into her industry—taking much better care of herself this time. She now looks for indications of prolonged stress as an early warning sign for burnout and makes changes when she needs to. Negin is currently a PR and communications consultant at the world-leading global agency Burson Cohn & Wolfe. She has also written a book called *Fight Smart and Dream Big*.

Tips for Handling Stress

Stress needs to be handled head-on, so here are a few practical ways to handle stress so we don't get overwhelmed by it:

- **TALK.** Whether we find a therapist, coach, accountability partner, family member, friend, or someone else, we all need someone we can trust and talk to. Talking to someone can help us work through stress and other emotional hardships we have.
- **MOVE.** There are thousands of studies that show that exercise helps us relieve tension and stress, and that it supports us in our overall well-being. My wife, Katie, can always tell when I've missed my workout. I'm just not the same person. Moving doesn't have to be a ten-mile run. It could be going for a walk, riding a bike, playing a sport, swimming, or doing anything physical. The key is to do what works for you.
- **UNPLUG.** Have you ever taken a break from TV, the news, and social media for even one day? If so, how did it feel? While it's good to know what's going on, the constant barrage of bad news, polarized viewpoints, and insulting social media posts can create significant stress. For many years, I've done news and social

media fasts—going for a day or days without accessing them—
and I always feel better when I do. Take a hiatus—a day or even
a week—and see if you can feel the difference.

- **BREATHE.** The main health benefits to breathwork are relaxation,
stress relief, and self-awareness. Breathing exercises can help us
stay present in the moment and calm ourselves down. For example, box breathing is an exercise where we inhale through the
nose, counting to four, hold the breath for four seconds, exhale
for four seconds, and hold the breath again for four seconds.
Another simple one is the 4-7-8 technique: breathe in for four
seconds, hold the breath for seven seconds, and breathe out for
eight seconds. Breathing can steady our heart rate and help us
feel less anxious.

Rest

We all make better choices when we're well rested. When you read the
word *rest*, what do you think about? If you're like most of us, you might
think of sleep. Dr. Saundra Dalton-Smith is a wellness expert, speaker,
and author who teaches about rest and recovery. According to Dalton-Smith, we confuse rest and sleep to our detriment. There are many
forms of rest, and sleep is only one of them. Here's a list:

1. **PHYSICAL REST**, which can be passive (sleeping or napping) or
active (restorative activities like yoga and massage).
2. **MENTAL REST**, which can include short breaks throughout the
day to remind us to slow down for a moment.
3. **SENSORY REST**, where we unplug from bright lights, screens,
noise, and conversations (whether in person or online).
4. **CREATIVE REST**, where we awaken our sense of wonder through
nature or art.

5. **EMOTIONAL REST,** which is having the time and space to freely express emotions without having to please someone else.
6. **SOCIAL REST,** where we take a break from socializing, particularly from those relationships that leave us feeling drained.
7. **SPIRITUAL REST,** which is the time and space to connect with a higher purpose in life, whatever that looks like for us.[10]

Rest is not laziness. It increases our effectiveness. The US Office of Disease Prevention and Health Promotion says that adults who get a minimum of seven hours of sleep each night are less prone to illness, able to maintain a healthy weight, think more clearly, have more positive social interactions, make better decisions, and are in an all-around happier mood than those who don't.[11] The same is true of all types of rest.

When Michael was fifteen, he backpacked through Europe. Somewhere along the way, he became very ill. He had to stop traveling and hunker down in the Loire Valley, France. He was used to the go-go-go mentality of a young traveler, and the sudden stop was a jarring experience. Forced to do nothing but rest for forty-eight hours, Michael realized—for the first time—that it was okay to be still. He didn't have to read or be productive every single moment. That experience still shapes how Michael views rest, particularly in a society that values constant productivity.

TAKE COMMAND

Stress is inevitable. While most people view it as a negative experience, the truth is that we need stress to keep us going. We wouldn't accomplish anything, not even basic functions like eating and bathing, without the benefit of eustress. The key is to not let stress overpower us. Remember, the negative experience of stress is more often related to the worry and anxiety about problems we face, rather than the problems themselves. If we can work to minimize our reactions to stress, we can use it to our advantage.

PRINCIPLE
Use stress to your advantage.

ACTION STEPS

- Instead of dwelling on the problem and getting dragged into a downward emotional spiral, use the problem-solving technique, and write down your answers.
  - **WHAT IS THE PROBLEM?** Separate the actual circumstances of the problem from your feelings and thoughts about it.
  - **WHAT ARE THE CAUSES OF THE PROBLEM?** Go to the root—what factors led to it?
  - **WHAT ARE THE POSSIBLE SOLUTIONS?** Write down every possible solution, no matter how drastic or ordinary they seem.

- **WHAT ARE THE BEST SOLUTIONS?** Consider the outcome—which solutions will give you the best possible result? Are there any solutions you can combine? As soon as you decide on the solutions that you think will work best, act on them.
- **CULTIVATE METHODS FOR RELIEVING STRESS.** Think about the things you do that bring you joy and help you relax. Make a list of them and make a point to incorporate at least one of those activities into your daily life. Some ideas include:
  - Talk to someone you trust.
  - Exercise every day.
  - Take breaks from TV and social media.
  - Try breathing exercises.
  - Rest.

8

BUILD RESILIENCE AND COURAGE

Inaction breeds doubt and fear. Action breeds confidence and courage.

—Dale Carnegie

Jenny Xu received the worst news of her professional life while standing in Times Square during a family vacation. Surrounded by crowds of people and flashing billboards, Jenny felt her phone vibrate. She looked down and saw a text from her only investor. Jenny's studio was working with a company to develop a social fitness game, so she called the investor immediately. When she answered, the investor said, "We need to talk. Your project is canceled. This is too expensive, and we're pulling our investment." Just like that, without any context or explanation, the funding for the game Jenny and her team had been designing for the last year was gone. Jenny stood in stunned silence in the middle of Times Square, frozen as the reality sunk in.

Jenny had a lot of experience in her field—she founded an independent game company when she was only sixteen, and the mobile games she's developed have over 9.2 million downloads. After completing a computer science degree at MIT, she cofounded a gaming studio called Talofa Games and won multiple awards—all before the age of twenty-five. Although Jenny knew that the gaming industry was cut-throat, she had never experienced that for herself. It felt like a forced exit—as if someone had packed her things and told her to leave her own apartment. Over the next few days, Jenny learned that the end of the relationship had a lot to do with external factors she couldn't control. The two companies hadn't been on the same page, and there had been communication issues. She talked to her mentors and learned that, while her investor ended the relationship suddenly and heartlessly, abrupt endings are common in her industry.

When she got together with her team the next week, she shared that they were in a tough position. She was emotional when she told the team that she would have to let half of them go. It was a very hard moment, but this was Jenny's wake-up call to trust herself. It would have been easy to curl up into a ball and ignore everything going on around her, but she found the strength and resilience to keep going.

She didn't know what was going to happen, so she thought about what she did know. She was only twenty-three, but she had been developing games for the better part of a decade. That knowledge helped soothe the sense of failure. She knew she wasn't alone—the team members who stayed were eager to take on the challenge. She felt tired and angry after hearing that the investor didn't believe in her vision. But she knew if she wanted her business to survive, she couldn't throw up her hands in defeat.

Jenny and her team got to work, and they realized that the game could launch sooner than if they had continued working with the investor, and Jenny was confident they could do it.

As a marathon runner, she was no stranger to exhaustion. "I think there's an element of being resilient in sports and exercise that carries over into the rest of life. If it feels like I'm dying in one race, it always ends, and I recover, and I'm stronger next time." She used that understanding to dig deep and find the resilience to keep going and the courage to keep her vision alive. As of this writing, her team is rebuilding their game, and it's set to release shortly.

Resilience and courage are closely related. Resilience is our ability to "bounce back" from adverse experiences and make something meaningful out of hardship. This is a critical topic, especially now, when our world faces so many challenges. Resilience is not turning to stone and muscling through life; it is facing down adversity with the goal of growing from your experiences.

Courage is the mental or moral strength to withstand danger, fear, or difficulty. Someone who is courageous would have the kind of character that keeps them from being afraid or intimidated easily. When we think about courage, we often think about the big heroic acts, the feats of daring and strength that we read about online or in history books. But courage is not just a big-moment act. It's a daily habit that we can cultivate. It's something we must commit to.

Both resilience and courage require strength, agility, and boldness— and they both require that we confront our fear. The development of courage and resilience is the culmination of all of the work we've done up to this point—everything from choosing the right thoughts and working with our emotions to dealing with stress and handling change helps us become strong over the course of our lives.

As Ryan Holiday writes in his book *On Courage*, "What is the source of cowardice? Fear. *Phobos*. It's impossible to beat an enemy you do not understand, and fear—in all its forms, from terror to apathy to hatred to playing it small—is the enemy of courage. We are in a battle against fear."

So how do we build courage and resilience during difficult or challenging moments?

1. Work with our emotions and choose uplifting thoughts.
2. Look backward to look forward.
3. Reinforce our faith in ourselves.

First, it's difficult to accurately assess a situation when we're flooded with emotions and fearful thoughts. We have to take the time to work through our emotions using the process in Chapter 3, "Work with Your Emotions," and then choose to let go of negative thoughts and replace them with uplifting ones.

Next, we need to look backward to understand how we will move forward. Think of a time when you overcame a difficult situation. What was the scenario? How hard was it? How did you feel? And most importantly, how did you get through it—what specific actions did you take, and what mindset did you have that helped you get through the situation? We've all faced hard times, and with a little reflection on our past resilience and courage, we might see that we're capable of persevering. Consider how you could use the same mindset or similar actions to get you through the present challenge.

One of the ways I was able to find courage to lead Dale Carnegie during the early days of COVID (discussed in Chapter 1, "Choose Your Thoughts") was to look back on one of my greatest challenges. When 9/11 hit in 2001, I feared my fragile startup would fail. We should have. We had just launched our first product and had very little revenue. A funding round we needed to survive looked all but impossible when a key investor backed out. If something didn't happen quickly, we would be forced to shut down in a matter of weeks. But somehow, we made it through those days. Through incredible belt-tightening, amazing teamwork to accelerate the launch of new products to bring in additional revenue, and the strong support of our existing investors, we made it through that experience. Plus, I learned that when people pull together with unyielding sacrifice and determination, they can get through anything. Thinking about that experience inspired me during the early days of COVID. It filled me with conviction. When I told our Dale Carnegie shareholders, board, and team members, "We will make it through this. We will do whatever it takes. Failure is not an option," I meant it. I came to believe that my past experiences had prepared me to lead in that very moment in time.

Finally, do something that will help you affirm your faith in yourself. You could write an affirmation for yourself that you can turn to frequently. You could talk with people who were with you when you got through the challenging situation. You might visualize your own success navigating perilous times. Whatever works for you, do it. Remind yourself of your strength, and rely on this success when you feel the fear and uncertainty resurface.

Fear isn't always obvious. Our fear can show up in subtle ways—avoiding or resisting having a difficult conversation with someone, pretending there aren't problems in a relationship or work situation. It can masquerade as procrastination or apathy. Our avoidance only causes the situation to fester because we refuse to deal with it.

Lea Gabrielle has worn many hats in her career—naval combat aviator, clandestine intelligence operative, journalist, and United States Special Envoy and Coordinator of the Global Engagement Center. But some of her most defining moments of service took place when she had to face extremely dangerous circumstances over and over—and when she had to commit to being courageous, knowing the consequences could be deadly. Lea flew the F/A-18C single-seat fighter plane, from a nuclear-powered aircraft carrier. While Lea was on a combat deployment, a more senior pilot whom she admired, named Lieutenant Commander Robert E. "Trey" Clukey III—a Top Gun graduate—was killed when his F/A-18C crashed while conducting a night training mission at sea. "We never found Trey, or his jet," Lea recalled. "He was an awesome guy and an awesome pilot." The aircraft carrier paused operations and held a formal memorial at sea with full military honors for Lieutenant Commander Clukey. "It was a tragic reminder to all of us that everything we do as carrier-based navy jet pilots, from catapult launch, to training, to our combat missions in Afghanistan, to our aircraft carrier landings, is extremely dangerous," Lea said. Once Clukey had been properly honored, the air wing quickly went back to regular operations, the pilots conducting notoriously dangerous takeoffs and landings, night and day, from a ship in constant motion.

Lea found the daily resilience and courage to face potentially deadly circumstances every time she took off. Commitment and focus helped her get through those nerve-racking moments. After completing her pre-flight briefing, she put her gear on, inspected the plane, climbed into the cockpit, and prepared all the systems. She knew that once she was hooked up to the launch catapult and gave the thumbs-up and salute, she was committing to both herself and her work. "Every single time, it takes courage to do it," Lea said. "I think that's when I realized who I was as a human. . . . I realized that every single time I had the opportunity to challenge myself and push myself forward, I needed to do it. You realize when you're in those moments that you're only as good as the last time you were challenged." As a result of Lea's ability to draw on her courage, she was able to continue with a distinguished career, including a deployment on the ground with SEALs in Afghanistan. In moments of doubt, she remembers the poem "Invictus" by William Ernest Henley: "I am the master of my fate, I am the captain of my soul."

In our experience, overcoming fear and finding your inner courage and resilience come down to a commitment to be emotionally courageous. Emotional courage is the willingness to feel your emotions and act at the same time. We can cultivate the ability to act thoughtfully, strategically, and powerfully . . . at the same time that we feel afraid.

It's not enough to just "get over" our fear. That's not realistic. We must learn to work with it. When we use the process for working with our emotions from Chapter 3, "Work with Your Emotions," we can identify some of the things that are causing us to feel afraid and do something about them. When we practice noticing where the fear arises in our bodies, we can learn how to experience fear without getting lost in it. Remember in the previous chapter when we talked about viewing our stress as helpful for us? We can do the same with fear—whatever physical sensations we experience when we're feeling nervous, uncertain, or afraid, we can reinterpret in a way that helps us. Beyond that, though, we must still learn to act when we feel fear. We must focus on the process of getting to where we want to go, not on whatever is standing in our way.

When Bina Venkataraman was a self-described "lowly novice reporter"[1] at the *Boston Globe*, she often felt intimidated by the people around her. She believed more in what other people said and thought than she did in herself. This included readers of the newspaper and naysayers who disagreed with what they published.

During one assignment, Bina learned about an offshore wind farm. This information inspired her so much that she took on a powerful senator from Massachusetts, the late Ted Kennedy. She wrote an in-depth story about his political efforts to stop the creation of that wind farm. The article ran on a weekend, and even though it was Saturday, Kennedy called nearly every single editor at the paper to complain. When each editor called Bina in turn, she told them the same thing—that she had the facts and statements to support what she wrote.

Bina was afraid. It might have been easier to back down in the face of accusations from one of the most powerful politicians in the country, but she chose to be courageous and stick to her guns. "That small, super unsexy moment in my career—answering calls about Ted Kennedy from editors—turned out to be pivotal. It was a moment when I stood up for myself. . . . Courage still doesn't come easily to me. But I've discovered that I can find it in myself when I know I am fighting a good fight," she said.

Her courage served her well. Bina later served as the director of global policy initiatives at the Broad Institute of MIT and Harvard from 2010 to 2019. She was the senior advisor to Eric Lander while he was the cochair of the President's Council of Advisors on Science and Technology. She went on to work in the White House as a senior advisor for climate change innovation.

For Bina, having a higher sense of purpose and a commitment to what she thought was right—to her values—kept her from backing down in the face of pressure.

Think about a challenge you are facing or that you have faced that requires you to have a high degree of strength. How did you handle that situation, and do you wish you could have handled it even better?

In our own Dale Carnegie research, we saw that highly resilient people usually maintained a positive attitude, felt confident in their abilities, coped well with challenges, recovered quickly from crises, and absorbed lessons from bad experiences that they could use in the future. People who have a high degree of strength and resilience ask themselves questions like "What can I learn from this? How can getting through this help me grow? What must I do right now to move forward? What happens if I focus on how bad this is for too long?"

We also saw perception play a big part in resilience: the most resilient people perceived the same event as less stressful than their less resilient colleagues. Just 16 percent from the high-resilience group who had experienced a challenging event said it resulted in a high level of stress, compared with 31 percent in the low resilience group. This shows that resilience is as much about how we perceive adversity as it is about how we react to it. Obviously, we want to be in the "resilient" group as often as we can, so we should start by questioning how we perceive a situation.[2]

After studying resilience at the University of Pennsylvania, Lucy Hone returned home to Christchurch, New Zealand, and started her doctoral research—just as massive earthquakes devastated the area. Lucy started working with her community to get them through the post-quake period. She thought this was the ultimate moment to put her research to work. Sadly, she was wrong.

Three years later, Lucy and her family were at Lake Ohau in the south of New Zealand when her daughter, Abi, decided to go for a car ride with Lucy's best friend, Sally, and her daughter, Ella. As they traveled down the road, a car sped through a stop sign and crashed into them, killing them all instantly.

Lucy was now on the other side of the equation—receiving advice from others about being resilient. And she didn't like what she was hearing. Lucy noticed that all the suggestions she received from others left her feeling like a victim who couldn't survive the drastic pivot in her life. She felt "powerless" and unable "to exert any influence" over her experience.[3]

Lucy thought what she needed was hope, and she wanted to have some control over her grieving process. So she turned her back on the advice she'd been given and focused on three strategies she had gleaned from her research of people who were able to persevere.

The first was that resilient people accept that suffering is part of life. They adopt a mindset that leaves room for the possibility that hard times will come. "Never once did I find myself thinking, 'Why me?' In fact, I remember thinking, 'Why not me? Terrible things happen to you, just like they do everybody else. That's your life now; time to sink or swim,'" she said. Lucy is right. Terrible things do happen and are, unfortunately, a part of life. Let's accept that we will face challenging times throughout our lives. We forget this, especially when we see the happy and perfectly planned moments shared on social media.

The second point was that emotionally strong people become very good at choosing where they place their attention. They choose to focus their thoughts and their attention on the things they can change, while accepting what they can't. When her emotions threatened to swallow her up, Lucy reminded herself of what she had to live for, starting with her two boys, who deserved fully present parents. She also thought about all of the social support they had and the love that helped them through. "Being able to switch the focus of your attention to also include the good has been shown by science to be a really powerful strategy," Lucy said.

The third insight she had was that emotionally strong people continually ask themselves, "Is what I'm doing helping or harming me?" This was Lucy's go-to question after the tragedy. She used it to decide whether to go to the trial of the driver and when she found herself poring over photos of her daughter. Lucy trained herself to avoid indulging in self-pity. She had to focus on whether her thoughts and actions would help or harm her, whether they were creating positive or negative experiences for her. Over time, these approaches helped her navigate her grief in healthier ways and find hope despite terrible tragedy.

Ryan Chen, paraplegic entrepreneur, is one of the most courageous and resilient people Michael and I have the pleasure of knowing. He has overcome incredible hardship and still manages to have a good attitude about life. Ryan spent his entire youth as a happy-go-lucky kid—energetic, athletic, and always up for adventure. When he found himself on the side of a mountain on a snowboarding trip at the age of nineteen, he didn't hesitate to take a massive jump. He flew high into the air, over-rotated, and landed hard on his back.

As he lay in the snow, Ryan knew that something was wrong—he couldn't feel his legs, and he couldn't get up. Despite a huge snowstorm, the ski patrol managed to get Ryan to a hospital. When he woke from the eight-hour surgery, the doctors told him that he had a serious spinal cord injury, and he would never walk again. Ryan lay in his hospital bed in stunned disbelief. He told himself they had to be mistaken. No matter what, he was determined to walk out of the hospital and prove everyone wrong.

Over the next six months, Ryan endured intense rehabilitation. He learned to sit up again, balance, and navigate a wheelchair. After he had undergone numerous unsuccessful surgeries, Ryan's outlook gradually darkened. "Everything I thought I knew about myself and my identity was stripped away," he said. He could think only of the things he could no longer do. Before his injury, Ryan had been extremely active—he practiced and competed in kendo martial arts, served as the captain of his high school cross-country team, and skied regularly. What was life going to be like if he couldn't walk?

After Ryan finally left the hospital, he went back to school, learned how to drive again, and got a job, but all he could think about was what he had lost. He took every painkiller imaginable, which led to two years of intense brain fog and opiate addiction. It took several years to get off the prescriptions, but once he did, his mind was finally clear, and Ryan felt like himself again. He started noticing the friends and family who had supported him since his accident. He realized how lucky he was to be alive. Most people in his situation wouldn't have gotten a second chance. Ryan began to apply himself more in school and reach for the same potential he knew he'd had before his accident. "I thought, 'Well, if I'm going to go through life, why half-ass it? Why not give it my best?'"

One day, Ryan's close friend from high school, Marcus, invited him to go on a trip. Marcus had been touring with incredible musicians like Coldplay and Mumford and Sons while making a documentary. At first, Ryan was hesitant. He hadn't traveled since his accident, but the idea was appealing. Marcus finally convinced him to go, and that trip shifted Ryan's perspective from a world of closed possibilities to a world of endless opportunities.

Once Ryan changed his perspective away from his old life and toward the future, he suddenly saw all the things he *could* do. Prior to his injury, Ryan had always wanted to run a marathon. He thought that was impossible after the accident. Then he learned about wheelchair racing and hand cycling. Within three weeks of working with a coach, he felt ready to try a marathon. "It was insane, but I ended up finishing! It took me four hours, and I was dying, but I was also hooked," he said.

With each new chance he took, he felt stronger and more capable. Every risk he took and succeeded in built his sense of self-efficacy. It wasn't long before he decided to take his drive and apply it to business. Because of his negative experience with prescription drugs, Ryan wanted to make a natural option that could give people energy and clarity in a safe and science-backed way. With his college friend Kent, Ryan cofounded Neuro, a company that blends gum and mints with functional nootropics and brain-boosting vitamins.

Ryan doesn't regret going off that jump, because he has learned so much in the process of reshaping and rebuilding his life and worldview. "If you feel like your back is against the wall and all opportunities are closed, take a moment to look around—other opportunities and doors will open up," Ryan said. "Just never give up."

After Ryan decided to focus on the parts of his life that he could control, his attitude changed for the better. He occasionally trains with the US Paralympics team, learned to scuba dive, and is in the process of becoming a licensed pilot. He didn't simply overcome his obstacles—his limitations helped him see the world in a new way and gave him a kind of strength he hadn't known he possessed.

TAKE COMMAND

Remember, building resilience and courage is the culmination of all of the work we've done up to this point. Our ability to be strong is a direct result of choosing the right thoughts, working with our emotions, cultivating confidence, embracing change, letting go of regrets, and dealing with stress. Although it can seem like life events are out of our control, we always have the option to choose how we react—with strength, courage, and resilience.

PRINCIPLE
Use hardships to build your inner strength.

ACTION STEPS
- Cultivate courage and resilience.
  - **WORK WITH YOUR EMOTIONS AND CHOOSE UPLIFTING THOUGHTS.**
    - Use the frameworks from Chapters 1 to 3 to soothe the way you're thinking and feeling about the situation.
  - **LOOK BACKWARD TO LOOK FORWARD.**
    - Think about a challenge you have faced in the past. What was the situation?
    - What did you do that showed courage, resilience, or strength?
    - What was your mindset at the time? What were your thoughts and emotions?

- ◦ What can you take from that past situation and use in the present?
- **REINFORCE YOUR FAITH IN YOURSELF.**
  - ◦ What action can you take right now to build emotional strength? Go do it.
  - ◦ Consider using an affirmation to help remind you that you are strong and capable.
- When you need to build your resilience, remember that highly resilient people do specific things that help them get through hard times.
  - **ACCEPT THAT SUFFERING IS PART OF LIFE.** Much like "cooperating with the inevitable," how can we get comfortable with the idea that life will throw us curveballs from time to time?
  - **CHOOSE WHERE TO PLACE YOUR ATTENTION.** We may not control what happens to us, but we can control where we put our focus. Decide now where you will put your concentration—on your goals and on the actions you can take.
  - **ASK YOURSELF, "IS WHAT I'M DOING HELPING OR HARMING ME?"** Ruminating on our fear or our emotions usually doesn't help. What tools can you use to move on from unhelpful actions during hard times in life?

PART II

TAKING COMMAND OF YOUR RELATIONSHIPS

Whether you consider yourself an introvert, an extrovert, or something in between, connecting with people authentically and respectfully is one of the most important skills you can have. When Michael and I reflect on our lives, we realize that the best parts of life involve relationships.

While the way we interact with other people varies across cultures, we can all agree that how we connect with others is vital. The nature of our close relationships changes over time. We might start out with friendships of convenience—people we meet through school or activities—and watch those connections fade as we age and grow apart. We might get to know others through our work. We hopefully build relationships that are meaningful and stand the test of time. Over the course of our lives, our relationships will evolve and change, but they will always require effort and attention.

In this section, we'll talk about the importance of cultivating connection with other people and what it means to build a strong relationship. We'll explore how to build trust, which is the foundation of any relationship (whether it's with our best friend or a coworker). Next, we'll tackle the dreaded c-word: *criticism*. Whether we're giving or receiving it, criticism is never fun. We'll walk through some scenarios and differentiate between criticism and feedback. Every relationship experiences discord. We can't control other people, but we can control ourselves, and we'll learn how to move through difficult conversations—often with challenging people—with more ease. Finally, we'll talk about how to see from another person's perspective and give practical tips on building empathy.

Once we learn to take command of our inner lives, we must do the same for our relationships. It's only by understanding ourselves that we can authentically connect and care for others, and it is only through building strong, mutually beneficial relationships that we can live a meaningful life.

9

GET CONNECTED

If you want others to like you, if you want to develop real friendships,
if you want to help others at the same time as you help yourself, keep
this principle in mind: Become genuinely interested in other people.

—Dale Carnegie

One reason Dale wrote *How to Win Friends and Influence People* is because
he was concerned about the number of people he met who didn't know
how to build strong relationships. Without these skills, people couldn't
progress in their careers or have healthy conversations with their families. Dale saw that people who could effectively interact and communicate with others have richer, fuller, happier lives. *HTWF* evolved out
of a set of principles that took up no more room than a postcard, then
grew to a leaflet, then a pamphlet, and, eventually, into a book. *HTWF*
is still a best-selling book more than eighty-five years later, which shows
that people still want to know how to connect with others. They want
to "win friends" and "influence people." Relationships are no less important (or challenging) than they were when Dale first emphasized the
value of deep and intentional connection with our friends, family, and
colleagues.

In *HTWF,* Dale wrote, "Dealing with people is probably the biggest
problem you face, especially if you are in business." He cited a prominent

study stating that "even in technical lines such as engineering, about 15 percent of one's financial success is due to one's technical knowledge and about 85 percent is due to skill in human engineering—to personality and the ability to lead people." Dale saw that while technical skill was important, "the person who has technical knowledge *plus* the ability to express ideas, to assume leadership, and to arouse enthusiasm among people—that person is headed for higher earning power."[1] This reality is as true today as it was in 1936. Even though nearly a century has passed since this study was done, getting along with other people is as important as ever. If we want to succeed, we need to learn how to work well with others.

If you've ever watched a two-year-old play with another child, you know that relationship skills are learned, not inherited. As adults, we often take our relationships for granted, which makes it easy to believe we've got this skill mastered. But in truth, the world evolves so quickly that the way we connect with others has to adapt, too.

But have you ever wondered what makes a relationship? Simply put, it is the way two people connect emotionally, mentally, and sometimes, in a familial way. The Latin translation of relationship is *necessitudo*, from the same root as *necessity*. We need these connections with others, but we notice that many people tend to think they can go it alone, that they don't need other people, and that they are better "doing things on their own." This could not be further from the truth.

Robert Waldinger is the head of the longest-running happiness study ever conducted. The Harvard team leading it now is the fourth generation of scientists to study what makes a happy life, and there have been three major findings.

First, social connections are good for us; conversely, loneliness kills. The study shows that those participants who are more connected to family, friends, and community are happier, physically healthier, and live longer. The second lesson is that it's not the number of friends we have but the quality of our close relationships that matters. While living with warm relationships is beneficial, living in constant conflict is bad for our health. The third lesson is that good relationships don't just protect our physical health but our brain health, as well. The study has shown that people who are in trusting relationships have sharper memories.[2] As Waldinger says in his TED talk, this wisdom is as "old as the hills." Why is it so hard, then?

> What we'd really like is a quick fix, something we can get that'll make our lives good and keep them that way. Relationships are messy and they're complicated and the hard work of tending to family and friends, it's not sexy or glamorous. It's also lifelong. It never ends. . . . Many of our men when they were starting out as young adults really believed that fame and wealth and high achievement were what they needed to go after to have a good life. But over and over, over these seventy-five years, our study has shown that the people who fared the best were the people who leaned into relationships, with family, with friends, with community.[3]

When I look at my life, a single common denominator for all my most impactful and important moments is my relationships. The people in my life give me joy and satisfaction, and they help me learn and grow. I hope I do the same for them. Relationships are not just "nice to have." Strong relationships help us live healthier, longer lives. A review of 148 studies determined that those of us with strong social ties are 50 percent less likely to die prematurely.[4] Friendships that help us feel cared for can act as a buffer against the effects of stress, too.[5] On the other hand, researchers have found that feeling disconnected and socially unsupported can lead to poor health outcomes, like higher rates of depression, decreased immunity, and higher blood pressure.[6] We need relationships for our mental, emotional, and physical health.

I've known Michael for over twenty years, and we've developed a strong friendship, though it was originally all about business. After I took the Dale Carnegie Course in 1995, I found that I wasn't using the principles as much as I wanted to, even though I had found them so impactful. So I developed a system and added it to my daily routine. Every day, I chose one principle to practice, an action step I'd take, and an inspirational quote on which I'd reflect. Eventually, I made a daily planner that standardized this content for one year.

After I had used this system for myself for a few years, a friend suggested that I contact Dale Carnegie Training and tell them about my planner. "Maybe this could be valuable to other Dale Carnegie Course graduates?"

"I don't know," I replied. "Big companies like that are probably inundated with ideas. Why would they listen to mine?"

"You never know. What have you got to lose?" I couldn't argue with that. I wrote a letter to Oliver Crom, Dale Carnegie Training's CEO, outlining my concept, and I sent it via FedEx, so he'd get it overnight. I waited a day and then called him. "Hello, Dale Carnegie Training," said a pleasant voice as I held the phone nervously. "I'd like to speak with Oliver Crom, please," I told the receptionist. "One moment," she said. To my dismay, the next thing I heard was "Hello, Ollie Crom." Wow, the CEO of Dale Carnegie Training took my call. . . . I was blown away. Ollie said he had read my letter and loved the idea. "I'd like to do a pilot," Ollie told me, "and I've got just the person to help lead this. My son, Michael, is one of our top executives. I'll talk with him, and then you and he can work together." That was the beginning of my relationship with Michael.

At first, Michael struck me as professional but quiet and a bit formal. We worked together to frame the pilot and test out the planner with two franchisees. I was interested in getting to know Michael better, so I began asking him questions. "Michael, tell me about yourself. What types of things do you like to do when you're not working?" I asked.

"The most important things in my life outside of work are my faith, family, and friends. I'm very active in my church and community."

"Really," I said. "Tell me more." Michael talked about his faith and how he started each day studying online Bible passages; about his wife, Nancy, and his two young children, Nicole and Alex; about how he got involved with Dale Carnegie and how excited he was about the impact the company had on individuals and organizations. As I listened, I realized we had much in common. My faith was also important to me, my wife was expecting our first child, and the Dale Carnegie Course had changed my life. Getting to know Michael as a person made our work together even more enjoyable.

While the franchise pilot was successful, Dale Carnegie Training did not move forward with the project at that time. It was only two years later, after I started my first company, that we began a global implementation of the initial pilot program. While Michael had been promoted and another senior executive was now leading our initiative, Michael and I stayed in touch, catching up during my trips to New York and at Dale Carnegie's annual conventions. I'd also call Michael from time to time to say hello, or vice versa. Each time we connected, I learned more about Michael, who he was and what was important to him. What had started initially as a business relationship was becoming more of a friendship.

Years later, when I was invited to enter the selection process for the next CEO of Dale Carnegie, I called Michael to get his thoughts. I said, "If you don't think this is a good idea, I won't pursue it. What do you think?" And he said, "It's a *great* idea." He advised me in the recruiting process, and I relied on his guidance.

Through my friendship with Michael, I've learned that building a strong relationship requires us to make time. It doesn't just happen— you have to invest time and energy into the relationship for it to flourish. Michael and I had a genuine desire to get to know each other, and we cultivated a sense of mutual trust and respect through our shared interests and values.

In contrast, too many people whom I've worked with in the past are mechanical in their interactions—they may want your business, but you can tell that they don't really care about you. Creating a genuine connection means that we have to get curious about the other person. Ask yourself, "What can I learn from this person? What do they really care about? What can I offer them?"

When we become genuinely interested in the people around us, we can actually enjoy our interactions instead of just getting through them. To be clear, we're not advocating that you pursue a friendship with every single person you meet. You don't have to have a relationship with everyone—in fact, you probably don't want to. Not everyone will align with your goals and values. Not everyone deserves your time. It's okay to choose carefully who you want to surround yourself with. But when you do choose, make the relationship with that person a priority in your life.

Like the fish who can't see the water, we don't realize the importance of our relationships until a challenge arises—like when we experience a loss of trust that makes repairing the relationship impossible, or great illness or death threatens to separate us from our loved one.

Andy Zinsmeister always thought that he would grow up and work alongside his parents, but that dream was threatened when his father, Bob, was diagnosed with cancer. At the time, Bob was the vice president of a team and Andy worked for him. Andy wanted to talk about the diagnosis with the employees and make sure people understood what his father was going through, but his father wanted something different. He didn't want flowers and pity, and he didn't want anyone fawning over him. He wanted to handle his business, avoid causing a distraction, and let the team operate normally.

Only twenty-two years old at the time, Andy didn't feel like he knew how to process his father's illness. His father had always been the one to pick him up during the difficult times of his life, and now Andy wanted to do the same for him. Before, their relationship had been the traditional parent-child one, with the parent taking most of the responsibility for the connection. But now, because Andy faced the possibility of losing his dad, he realized how important his dad was to him and that he wanted to take more responsibility for their relationship.

Every day, Andy focused on connecting with his father in a small way by asking how he was doing or asking to hear a story about his life that Andy hadn't heard before. Sometimes Andy asked questions about what it was like to raise him. Knowing that their time together might be limited, Andy wanted to truly know his father before it was too late. "I decided to really be intentional about strengthening that relationship with him. Some days, he did better than others. Some days, he needed to talk. Some days, he just needed a head nod and to know that I was there with him," Andy said.

Bob eventually won his battle with cancer, and he and Andy now have an even stronger relationship because of it. Andy intentionally cultivated his connection with his dad because he realized how important it was to show him the same love and care that his father had given him. "I strongly believe in the power of taking command, whether it be of your own internal struggles or relationships or a change that needs to happen. It starts with a step: bravery," Andy said.

Five Ways to Build a Great Relationship

Building relationships is one of those nebulous goals that we don't always know how to pursue on a practical level. Michael and I thought about the factors that have been present in all of our most meaningful relationships and gathered them into five pieces of advice. Committing to even one (or more) of these approaches will help you get to know people authentically and show others that they matter to you.

BE WARM. Warmth is an underrated quality. Vanessa Van Edwards, lead investigator at her human behavior research lab, Science of People, and author of two books on human behavior, teaches that highly charismatic people show a mix of warmth and competence.[7]

Building relationships isn't just about being credible—it's about showing that you are emotionally safe and trustworthy.

What does it mean to be warm? Being warm often means being open and friendly. This seems like an obvious first step, but it bears repeating. Showing that you're open means showing it with your body language, facial expressions, and tone of voice. Think about the way you interact with a person in the first few moments. Do you smile? Do you show signs that you're listening, like nodding in agreement? Do you raise your eyebrows or mirror the other person's cues? Research has shown that 55 percent of communication is nonverbal, so the way we present ourselves in a situation is almost more important than the things we say.[8]

LISTEN. Listening well isn't simply not talking while someone else speaks. To listen well, we must open our minds to hear what they are saying—without planning what we will say next. Asking follow-up questions to gain a deeper understanding also shows that you're paying attention. Being patient with another person while they speak is also important. Half the battle of connecting with someone is learning how to listen to them so well that you can hear the subtext behind the words and offer whatever support they need but might not be able to ask for.

As Dale wrote, intent and focused listening is one of the highest compliments we can pay someone.

FIND COMMON GROUND. People build connections with others based on common interests, hobbies, professions, and values. When we're in the early stages of getting to know someone, common ground is where we can connect with each other. But finding common ground isn't an approach reserved only for a new relationship. We can use this technique when our relationships fade and we need to reconnect and bring them back to life. We can also use common ground when we inevitably hit a rough patch in our relationships. When we struggle, we can ask ourselves what we still have in common with that person and in what ways we still see eye to eye.

SHOW GENUINE CARE. Showing genuine care often means that we need to go beyond the vague and general greeting "How are you?" which usually gets the rote response "I'm fine, thanks." When we genuinely care about someone, we make it clear that we can talk openly and vulnerably about whatever is happening in life. We make space for the hard and heavy stuff as much as we make space for the things we get to celebrate. Showing genuine care often looks like asking questions that go deeper and making time to be with that person.

GIVE HONEST AND SINCERE APPRECIATION. Dale wrote, "Here is a gnawing and unfaltering human hunger. . . . The desire for a feeling of importance is one of the chief distinguishing differences between mankind and the animals."[9] People crave the feeling of appreciation. They want to know they matter. When you take the time to tell the people you care about—whether you've known them for days or a lifetime—that they make a difference in your life, you reaffirm their inherent value.

One of Michael's closest friends, Yesenia Aguirre, was a schoolteacher for seventeen years, and in her spare time, she now drives for Uber. But Yesenia is not simply an Uber driver. She is a beautiful example of someone who uses all five ways to build a relationship with someone. She makes it her job to uplift her passengers. "I have a captive audience," she says. "They're not going anywhere because they need me to take them to the next destination. What can I do to make them happy when they leave my car? What can I do to bring hope?"

First, she greets them warmly by using their name. She notices that so many of them are surprised already by hearing their name and the friendly way in which she says it. Then she compliments them. "People love to be complimented, and it opens up conversation really quickly."

Sometimes her passengers will notice that her profile says she was a teacher, and they'll ask her why she drives overnight. She takes the opportunity to share her story—she quit teaching because of her mom's health problems; she wanted to take care of her full-time. "That further breaks the ice because they see that a person is willing to sacrifice their life and their future and their dreams to help with their parents. And that kind of gets people to talk more personally about their life," she says.

Once, she picked up a hedge fund executive who shared with her that he was miserable—his work was top-notch, but his relationships were almost nonexistent. He felt he had little to look forward to in life. Yesenia listened quietly as he shared that he thought about jumping off of a building and ending his life.

Yesenia believes that if we are alive, then we have purpose. She told the executive so and then suggested that the next morning, he should look up St. Jude Children's cancer ward, or go to the Boys & Girls Club to help out. "You need to get out of your head," she told him. He listened to every word she said, then responded, "Thank you! I feel like I just went to therapy. I feel so much better."

Yesenia recently picked up a man who was going to serve ten years in federal prison a week from when they met. She asked him what happened, and he told her that four days prior, he had been convicted for selling drugs. It was the biggest bust on Long Island to date, the man told her.

He told her how he became involved with the drug trade after an accident where he fell off scaffolding and hurt his back. A friend of his gave him Vicodin. The man soon became addicted to it and then, in the quest for more of it, decided to sell it. One thing led to another, and it became his life. He told Yesenia, "I tried to do right, but the mortgage had to be paid, the car had to be paid. If I tried to do right and stopped dealing, then I got caught up in all those things, and the pressure got too high," he said. No matter how many times he tried to stop, he kept falling back on his drug trade.

The morning that he was arrested, he prayed and told God that if he was supposed to get out of the drug trade, then God would have to take him out completely. In a strange way, his prayer was answered.

Yesenia told him that whatever time he spent in prison, he should focus on going to school and planning what he wanted to do when he was released.

Before she dropped him off, Yesenia and her passenger prayed together. She gave him her number so he could call if he needed anything, and he said, "You have no idea, you just messed me up." Yesenia laughs whenever she hears this because it's what her passengers say when they are moved to tears by their connection. Yesenia later received a call from the man's mother, thanking her for her compassion toward her son.

Yesenia's approach to connection with compassion leaves all her passengers in a better place after riding with her. She turns an ordinary interaction into an extraordinary part of their day. These may sound like temporary connections, but Yesenia has turned many of her onetime passengers into friends because of her caring approach to building connections.

Relationships in a Digital Age

Even though we live in the age of effortless digital connection, it's gotten more difficult to foster deep, personal relationships. "Social media has given us this idea that we should all have a posse of friends, when in reality, if we have one or two really good friends, we are lucky,"[10] said author Brené Brown. Members of Gen Z spend as much as nine hours a day on screens, with texting or social media being their primary forms of contact with their friends.[11] Jean Twenge, psychology professor at San Diego State University, found in her research that "in the late 1970s, 52 percent of 12th-graders got together with their friends almost every day. By 2017, only 28 percent did. The drop was especially pronounced after 2010 . . . just as smartphone use started to grow." Rates of depression and loneliness skyrocketed in teens and young adults after 2012 and have only grown since.[12] While digital communication can be a gift for people who can't be physically present with each other, the research shows that social media is no substitute for face-to-face interaction.

Shortly after Rae Giordano gave birth to her daughter, she was exhausted but craving connection. "It was hard to talk with friends, though—I felt stuck in the cycle of breastfeeding, changing diapers, taking care of myself, and trying to sleep when I could. I felt like I had no time or energy for real conversation," she said. Though she had never been a big fan of social media before, she started scrolling more and more. The habit slowly snuck up on her until she realized she was even scrolling in the wee hours of the night to pass the time while her daughter fed. It gave her the sense of feeling connected because she could see what other people were doing.

"It worked for a while until I realized I hadn't spoken to anyone in real life other than my partner for well over a week," she said. That's when it dawned on Rae that the sense of connection she felt on social media was false. "It was a one-way street. I wasn't talking or connecting directly with anyone, and no one knew how I was really doing, even if I commented on someone else's post." Worse yet, because of that false sense of connection, she had neglected her real friendships. Rae decided to remove the Facebook app from her phone and only allowed herself to use the platform when she was on her desktop—and only for a certain amount of time. Then, she wrote out a list of the relationships she wanted to strengthen and decided that every time she felt the urge to get on social media, she would text someone on the list instead. Finally, she made in-person plans with friends at least once a week. Within a week, Rae felt a difference in her mood and in her relationships. She was actually connecting with people and contributing to the relationship. "Spending time with friends was worth far more than any time I could've spent on social media," she said.

TAKE COMMAND

Our relationships make life richer and more meaningful, and they help us accomplish our greatest goals in life. When we approach them with intention, we can build relationships that serve those around us and help us live the kind of life we dream of. The key is to take conscious action to nurture those relationships.

PRINCIPLE

Make people a priority.

ACTION STEPS

- **TAKE INVENTORY.** Think about the five people you care about most. Are your relationships with them as strong as you would like them to be? Why or why not?
  - What do you think life would be like if you didn't have those relationships?
- What's one thing you could do today that would strengthen each of your relationships with the five people you love most? Remember to consider the following:
  - **SHOW APPRECIATION.** What can you say or do to let them know what they mean to you?
  - **FIND COMMON GROUND.** Connect with them through shared interests.
  - **BE WARM.**

- **SHOW GENUINE CARE.** How can you show them that you care for them? What actions can you take today?
- **LISTEN.** Think about the last time you checked in with them to see how they are doing. Everyone goes through hard times—let them have as much time as they need to tell you how life is going for them.
- What actions could you take on a daily basis that would help you build stronger relationships? Build those actions into your daily routine.

10

CREATE TRUST

Be more concerned with your character than with your reputation, for your character is what you are, while your reputation is merely what others think you are.

—Dale Carnegie

Miriam Duarte, a master trainer at Dale Carnegie Germany, was brimming with enthusiasm as she looked at the participants in her session who were returning for the second of two days of general training. "Welcome back!" Miriam said with a broad smile. "In a moment, we are each going to stand up and give a two-minute talk about what happened yesterday when you applied one of the human relations principles we discussed in class. Who has a question?" Seeing none, Miriam invited to the front of the room the first participant, who shared her experience from the prior day.

One by one, each person went up, did the same, and sat back down to the sound of applause. After half an hour, everyone had spoken except for one woman who sat quietly in the back corner of the room. When Miriam called her, the woman refused to stand up. "I'm sorry," she said. "I just can't do this. I'm terrified of speaking in front of others." Miriam thought to herself, "I absolutely want to respect her wishes, but I wonder if this could be an opportunity for her to grow." Miriam saw that the woman didn't trust her or the other participants in the room and did not feel safe. "How about this," Miriam asked. "Would you be okay staying seated and just having me ask you a few questions? You don't have to if you don't want to."

"I guess I could do that," the woman replied hesitantly. Miriam gently asked a series of questions, to which the woman quietly replied. After her "interview-talk" was over, her peers erupted into loud applause to show their support.

The session continued, and at the end of the day, it was time for another short talk. One participant after another came up and shared an insight they had learned in the class. When reflecting on this moment, Miriam said, "I was curious to see if the woman would get up in front of the class this time, and I was careful not to make her feel uncomfortable or to break her trust."

When it was the woman's turn, Miriam started with praise and recognition for everything she had seen in the woman that day. The applause was enthusiastic yet again, and Miriam watched to see what she would do. The woman looked at the faces around the room, hesitated for a moment, then stood and walked to the front of the room. She began to speak. "This morning, I was so close to running out of the room because I couldn't imagine myself standing up here and talking to you folks. When I was in high school, I got pregnant. I was bullied and judged, and I didn't want to be around anyone, let alone stand in front of a room and talk in front of a large group. I'll be honest, this is terrifying for me right now. But I'm grateful, and I thank you because today I had the chance to be courageous for the first time in my life." When she finished, her peers thundered with applause and gave her a standing ovation.

Miriam knew that if she had forced the woman earlier, she wouldn't have been able to build the trust that eventually enabled her to stand up and speak on her own. Miriam had to help her see that she was safe, and that everyone wanted her to succeed. "This is a key experience that reminds me how important it is to respect people's boundaries. Everybody has reasons for the ways they behave, and who am I to judge them? All I want for people is to unfold their potential, and I learned that I can support that through building trust," she said.

While there are dozens of different ways to think about trust, Michael and I think of it as a firm belief that a person or thing is reliable. When we trust ourselves, another person, or an object (like a car, computer, or device), we feel we can rely on the character, ability, strength, or truth of that person or thing. Trust is the foundation of all positive relationships. Our ability to gain the trust of other people plays out in boardrooms and family rooms, on sports teams and in relationships around the world. It's multifaceted, intangible, and hard to define, yet it's crucial to every relationship we cultivate.

Every interaction we have with another person carries some level of risk and reward. The need for trust goes to our core humanity, safety, and self-preservation. Renowned developmental psychologist Erik Erikson called trust "the first task of the ego," and wrote that our ability to put trust in the people around us is fundamental to forming relationships and functioning in the world.[1] From our earliest days as humans, we have had to assess whether someone is going to hurt us or help us. This is why Dale's principles are so focused on building trust and respecting the dignity of the other person,

Let's be clear: it's possible to be in relationship with people we don't trust. Trust isn't critical for every single relationship to work, but it is necessary for the relationship to *thrive*. Both Michael and I have worked with people we didn't trust. It was necessary at the time—we don't always get to choose our colleagues. Neither one of us can say we felt good about the situation, but these were functional relationships centered around work. For mutually beneficial, life-giving relationships, trust is the foundation.

Sometimes it's not easy to trust other people because we've been hurt in the past. Especially deep hurt and pain can cause us to put walls up and keep people out. As much as that might feel like a solution, we don't do ourselves or anyone else any good if we can't learn to let people in. We need to take chances.

In our Dale Carnegie Courses, we use the trust equation, which looks like this: trust = personal credibility + empathy. People around us need to trust our credibility and our ability to emotionally connect with them. Trust builds when we consistently show integrity. It's not a onetime thing—strong trust in a relationship requires action and effort to support it. We can never assume we have someone else's trust if we haven't done the work to build it.

Trust plays a part in cultivating our communities—for example, our collective lack of trust in the media causes us to question everything we hear. Is what I'm hearing true? Does the person, site, or network reporting the "news" have an agenda? If so, how can I rely on *anything* they say? Lack of trust has real consequences on the grand scale. According to current research, every continent has high- and low-trust regions. Low-trust areas tend to have less philanthropy, more crime, shorter life spans, and big gaps between high- and low-income households.[2] This is what happens when there is no trust in a community. What happens when trust is broken in our personal relationships?

Ani and John were having dinner at their favorite taco place. It had been a long time since she had seen him, and she had been looking forward to the conversation. As they talked about their lives and caught each other up on the past few months, they also talked about some of their other classmates. "How's Meredith?" John asked. "Do you miss being roommates with her?"

"Ha! Hardly. She complained about everything—the other day, we had lunch and she told me that Beth was gaining weight, and when I told her I was going to see you, she said, 'He's so ambitious, he'd go to any lengths to get ahead.'" Ani hadn't thought what Meredith said was that bad. John *was* ambitious, after all, and it was one of her favorite things about him. But as she looked up from her meal, she could see that he was hurt by Meredith's words and the fact that Ani and Meredith had been talking about him behind his back. "Why were you guys talking about me like that? I thought she was my friend," he said. The rest of their evening was a little more tense than Ani would have liked it to be, but she hoped it would pass, and John would soon forget about the incident.

Well, Ani was wrong. The next day, Meredith called her—and she was infuriated with Ani. John had called and confronted Meredith about what she had said. "Ani, I only say those things to you because you're one of my closest friends. Why would you repeat that to John?!" Ani felt like she'd truly overstepped with both of her friends, and though she apologized to the both of them, it took time to earn back their trust over the next few months. An apology without correction can do more harm than good when it comes to trust.

When we break trust in a relationship, those we care about might feel a sense of betrayal, even if we never intended to hurt them. They might feel doubt, suspicion, and the need to protect themselves, which causes them to hold back from the relationship by being reserved or avoiding us altogether. This is why we should consciously work on building trust in our relationships. We can't expect a person to be vulnerable and open if they don't trust us. We wouldn't be open with a person *we* didn't trust. A customer won't buy from a business if they don't trust that they'll get the outcome they want. A supervisor won't promote or assign responsibility to an employee if they don't trust the employee can get the job done. Two people can never be intimate if there is no trust in a romantic relationship.

The Importance of Being Vulnerable

If we trust someone, that means we're comfortable being vulnerable with them and vice versa. Being vulnerable means that we are open and that our defenses are down. In many contexts, vulnerability is seen as a bad thing. We might use a phrase like "vulnerable to an attack," or "you've left yourself vulnerable," as a way of saying that we're in a position of weakness. We use the words "vulnerable people" to talk about those who can't defend themselves. It's no wonder that vulnerability has a bad reputation.

But vulnerability is a key to trust. We can't truly build deep trust until we can let our guard down. Our ability to be vulnerable impacts our authenticity, believability, and our relatability. Life is largely about fostering connections with other people, and one of the most important ways we create such a bond is by channeling and embracing our true selves. Sometimes that means putting ourselves out there and risking how people will respond.

It was June 2015, and I had just been named president and CEO of Dale Carnegie Training. Most of our organization is franchised, meaning that individual business owners represent Dale Carnegie in territories around the world. The franchise owners' association had invited me to speak for the first time before their members. Making a strong impression was vital to me. "Will they like me? Will they trust me? Dale Carnegie people are among the very best presenters in the world; what if my speech doesn't meet their standard? What if I bomb?" Plus, three members of our Dale Carnegie board of directors, including Michael, would be there to introduce me. The night before my talk, I lay awake in my hotel room, thinking through my presentation, barely sleeping. "Well, I've got one more thing to worry about now," I thought. "Everyone is going to see dark bags under my eyes in the morning."

As I stood before a packed ballroom the next morning, I started warmly, standing tall, smiling, and looking out over the audience. I talked about how much Dale Carnegie had meant to me and how I appreciated our franchisees and their dedication to helping others. I then moved on to my vision for the company and the need for us to work together effectively as "One Carnegie." I implored those in attendance to partner with me to reactivate our brand so that we could reach more people, especially younger people, than ever before. And then I shared the gut-wrenching decision my wife and I had made to move our family from Michigan, our lifelong home, to New York, leaving behind our elderly parents and our seventeen-year-old daughter who would be staying with close friends in Michigan so she could finish her senior year of high school. I did this, I said, because "I am all in for Dale Carnegie." And I continued: "I went to my wife, and I said, 'Katie, if I get this offer, and we take it, it's going to mean moving our family. We've never lived any place other than Michigan.' And my wife . . ." Then something happened that I hadn't planned, something that I never, ever would have wanted to do before any audience. I became emotional. As hard as I tried, my words were caught in my throat, and I couldn't speak. Instead, I looked down, my eyes welling up, and removed my glasses so I could wipe away the tears with a Kleenex I had fortunately stuffed into my pocket earlier that day. Thankfully, someone in the audience came to my rescue, as only an experienced Dale Carnegie trainer can do, and broke the silence with a question: "So what did she say?" Everyone laughed, and so did I. That moment enabled me to regain my composure. I replied, "She said, 'I'm all in.'"

At the end of my speech, I was stunned when our franchise owners jumped to their feet in a standing ovation and warm applause. I had been concerned that showing vulnerability would make me appear weak. Instead, person after person said it made me human to them. In my speech, shouldn't I have demonstrated strength instead of choking up? Sure, showing strength is important, but it was my openness and vulnerability that helped me connect with the people in the audience. It was not contrived—I didn't know I would get emotional—but I let my feelings show rather than cover them up. Emotional vulnerability isn't weakness. In that moment, I trusted the audience enough to let my authentic self show, and doing that allowed all of us to have a deeper connection to both me and the company. Even years later, people still talk about that speech and how it changed their view of me as a leader—for the better.

One of my favorite writers and leadership coaches, Patrick Lencioni, author of *The Five Dysfunctions of a Team*, writes about two different kinds of trust. The first kind is "predictive" trust, where we guess how another person will act based on what we know about their previous actions. For example, if your friend is always late, you would predict that they will be ten minutes late for your next lunch appointment, even though they insist they'll be there on time.

The other kind is "vulnerability-based" trust, where we feel able to be "emotionally naked" with each other. For example, if you're in a meeting and someone asks you a question, your immediate response might be to find any answer, even if it's mediocre, rather than admit that you don't have one. It would be far more vulnerable to simply say, "I don't know." Or let's say you've made a mistake with someone you care about. Your first response might be to get defensive and explain all the reasons why you did what you did. The vulnerable response would be to open up and say, "I made a mistake. I'm sorry," and then follow that statement with actions that show you're genuinely sorry and want to do better next time.

Undermining Trust

So what destroys trust? First, people usually expect that when they share something with us, we will keep it in confidence. When we repeat what they say in a way that hurts them or their relationships, they might feel betrayed and question our motives. What if we thought about the things people tell us as being subject to "the attorney-client privilege"? When I was a practicing lawyer, I was ethically bound to never share anything my clients told me (with some very limited exceptions, such as if a client said they were going to commit a crime . . . which fortunately never happened). This way, my clients could be completely open and truthful with me. If I had violated that privilege, I would have lost my license to practice law—and my livelihood. When I first learned about the attorney-client privilege, I remember saying to myself, "What if I applied this rule to all of my communications? What if people who shared things with me confidentially knew that I wouldn't disclose those things to anyone?" When friends approached me with delicate or personal information, I'd say right up front, "I want you to know I am not going to tell anyone what you share with me. I'm going to act as though there's 'attorney-client privilege,' even though there's not really—but I want you to know what you tell me is safe." For nearly thirty years, I've applied this principle to my relationships, and it's helped me develop deep trust with others. Tennis player Arthur Ashe once said, "Trust has to be earned, and should come only after the passage of time."[3] Because I keep what they say private, I have earned the trust of the people in my life.

Second, inconsistency erodes trust. Have you ever had a boss who tells you one thing one day and something different the next day? Or maybe they make vague promises about a promotion, but then cancel the meeting every time it's due to come up for discussion. Saying one thing and doing another shows a lack of integrity and makes it hard to trust that person. Even if it's unintentional—maybe they're forgetful or unorganized and don't remember what they've said from day to day—it causes people to wonder if that person will follow through.

Third, failing to listen to and communicate with the people around us leads to a lack of trust, but it often can be restored when we do. Katie Dill joined Airbnb when it was still a small company. There were ten people on the design team, and she was ecstatic to be a part of it—it was a dream job for her. "During the interviews, I learned a lot about what the company and the team needed. The design team had very low engagement scores," Katie said. "It was clear there was friction between the designers, engineers, and product managers, and the team wasn't working together as well as it could."

She was eager to do well, so she set about making changes right away. "I thought things were going well—change was happening. But about a month in, I got an invite on my calendar. Five of the ten designers wanted to meet with me. Somebody from HR was on the invite, too," she said. It was not a good sign.

Katie went into the meeting not really knowing what was going to happen. When she walked into the room, her team each had a stack of paper in front of them. "They sat me down and proceeded to take turns reading all the things that they didn't like about what I was doing and my leadership," she said.

While her emotions were welling up, and she was becoming increasingly defensive in her mind, Katie paused, kept her composure, and thought about Dale. "I remembered how Dale Carnegie wrote about how our instinct in a moment like that is to correct people when we disagree with them. But he also wrote that every time we call someone out, we bring the conversation to a defensive place, and no one is better off. I wanted to tell them how they got it wrong, but I listened instead. As hurtful as it was—and it was probably one of the scariest moments in my leadership career—it was an unbelievably powerful learning moment. It was clear from their words that I hadn't earned their trust. They didn't know I cared for them, believed in them, and sought out their best interest. I had moved fast to make changes and hadn't taken enough time to get to know them. Essentially, I came in swinging when I should have come in listening."

Katie took this learning moment seriously and immediately set out to build greater trust with the team. She spent more one-on-one time with each of her colleagues to learn more about them and get their input on how to move forward. "Showing care and listening were fundamental to the shift in the company," she said.

In just a few months, Katie's work with the team paid off, and soon the design department had one of the highest engagement scores in the company. When she left Airbnb to work at Lyft, she did it right the second time—she came in listening and building trust.

Although trust is critical to building solid relationships, it is fragile, making it hard to build and easy to break. When we're not careful with the trust others place in us, we can hurt our relationships. In their book *Connect*, Stanford professors Carole Robin and David Bradford tell the story of how they almost lost the professional relationship they had spent years building with each other. David had been Carole's mentor. They approached problems differently, but they could usually agree on common goals and settle arguments quickly.

When David decided to stop teaching one of his courses, the school asked Carole to take over—but she had requests. Carole knew how hard David had worked in that position, and now that it was her turn, she wasn't going to be taken for granted, too. She wanted the "course" to be called a "program" because she believed it would lead to more funding and support, and she wanted a specific title that better reflected the duties of that job. Stanford turned down both requests. Carole was furious and told David what had happened.

"Carole, why are you pushing so hard for the program and title? I just don't get what's the big deal," David said.

"The big deal is that I'm going to have to fight the very battles you are fighting right now. Without the recognition I'm asking for, I don't think I'll be successful," she said. While David agreed that it was a tough job, he didn't think this was a hill they needed to die on. He brought up Carole's request at his next meeting with school leadership, but when they asked him if her requests were necessary, he said, "Well, not getting these things certainly makes her job harder, but she can do it."

Carole felt betrayed and misunderstood when she found out what David said. "If the situation had been reversed, I would have gone to bat for you in an instant," she told him. Looking back on that conflict, Carole said, "I wasn't sure I'd ever be able to trust him again." They still had to work together, so they did what they had to and barely spoke outside of work.

Months later, the two sat down and talked about their relationship. Carole was still mad, and David didn't understand why. "It makes me really nervous to think I might not know where the next land mine is going to be with you," David said. Long before Carole had stopped trusting David, he had struggled to trust her. It became obvious that trust had failed on both sides.

After talking for several frustrating hours, they got to the core issue. They could only resolve their conflict once they were willing to voice their real emotions. At one point, David was able to empathize with Carole and said, "I'm seeing what has been going on for you, maybe for the first time. And I'm sorry." This helped Carole finally feel emotionally understood. "Our issues were highly entangled. . . . Even though we explored these issues in much greater depth and gained a clearer understanding of why each of us had responded as we had, everything was not all wrapped up in a neat bow," they wrote. They still had more work to do, but they had restored enough trust that they could rebuild their relationship.

A genuine effort to restore trust will go a long way. It's a process that takes honesty, admitting our mistakes, and an environment where others feel they can do the same.

So how do you know if you don't have someone's trust? Look for behavior and body language that show disconnection or unhappiness, such as guarded communication, in your workplace or friend group. Are people close-lipped around you? Is there tension or uneasiness? Are people acting cynical or suspicious? If you're talking with someone who seems defensive, it's a strong sign that they might not trust you.

If you know that you've lost someone's trust, try these:

1. **PUT YOUR EGO ASIDE.** Think about how to approach them openly and show your vulnerable and authentic self, especially if you are an authority figure or leader in their lives.

2. **TAKE RESPONSIBILITY FOR YOUR PART IN BREAKING THEIR TRUST.** It helps to look at your assumptions and how they affected your actions. Reflect on the role that you played in the situation.

3. **MEET AND TALK PRIVATELY WITH THEM TO SHARE YOUR REFLECTIONS.** Ask for their perspective, keep an open mind, and listen. As much

as possible, put yourself in their place—and hear what they have to say without judgment.

4. **ASSESS NEEDS.** Find out what that person needs from you to repair broken trust and share what you need from them. Listen and check to make sure you both understand each other. Consider meeting regularly to talk about progress.

5. **LET YOUR ACTIONS SPEAK FOR YOU.** Be vigilant about upholding your end of the deal. The old adage that "actions speak louder than words" should be your guide.

It's easy to feel defensive or insulted when we discover someone doesn't trust us. Our fight-or-flight mode can kick in pretty quickly. This is an opportunity to challenge ourselves to see things not just from our point of view, but more objectively. What has it been like for you when you've had to interact with someone you didn't trust? What do you wish they had said to you that would have helped you trust them more? We won't get it right every time, but what's important is that we keep trying. Appreciate the highs and lows of each journey—even if you didn't see them coming.

Psychological Safety

Trust comes into play within groups, too, which is referred to as the degree to which we feel "psychologically safe." As trust is critical to personal relationships, psychological safety is critical for an organization. Psychological safety is based on the perceived consequences of taking an interpersonal risk—sharing an opinion, speaking the truth, raising a difficult issue, or asking a question. If you find yourself afraid of appearing stupid, incompetent, negative, or disruptive for speaking up—whether in a meeting at work or with your family—you might feel psychologically unsafe. But if, on the other hand, you feel confident that others will receive your views openly, you might feel psychologically safe.

David Barrios is the CEO of HPC, a wholesale hardware tools distributor based in Guatemala. As a newly promoted leader, the last thing anyone would like to do is to ask how they're failing—but that's exactly what David did, and he created psychological safety in doing so.

In a leadership meeting, David decided to conduct an exercise designed to help everyone see the value of vulnerability-based trust, which he believes is the basis for working together. The exercise came from Lencioni's *The Five Dysfunctions of a Team* (which we mentioned earlier in this chapter), and the gist is this: each member of the team hears constructive feedback regarding (1) the single most important contribution they make and (2) the one area they must improve upon or eliminate for the good of the team.

When his turn came, David felt exposed after hearing the feedback— it was almost unanimous that he needed to be more empathetic. David later held one-on-one meetings with each person who was in the meeting to ask for more feedback and guidance about how he could improve.

"Of course, it was not easy to hear the message so loud and clear of where I was failing, but it was also great to have such clarity about what I needed to work on. The feedback I got was delivered in a very candid way and with a clear intention to help both me and the group dynamics, which is what our goal was—to be a better team!" David said. In any position, it might feel safer to act tough and under control. No matter what our position, growth requires that we listen to what people have to say. "I trusted my colleagues enough to be vulnerable with them and ask for their help, even when I was the CEO—or let me correct that, *especially* because I was the CEO—and they helped me in more ways than I could have imagined. I can confidently say that because of them, I came out the other side of those one-on-ones as a better person and a better leader," said David. The trust had to go two ways, too—the team had to believe that it was safe to give David their open and honest feedback.

TAKE COMMAND

Trust takes years to build and moments to break, and yet it is the foundation of all good relationships. We don't often think about how or why we trust the people who are closest to us, but no relationship can flourish without trust. When we think about building or strengthening relationships, trust has to be the first element we think about.

PRINCIPLE

Be yourself to build trust.

ACTION STEPS

- **THINK ABOUT THE ROLE TRUST PLAYS IN YOUR LIFE.** Who in your life do you trust the most? Who do you trust the least? Think about what these people do to bolster or break your trust. How do they treat and speak to you?
- **NOW THINK ABOUT HOW YOU SHOW UP IN YOUR RELATIONSHIPS.** Are you trustworthy? What do you do that builds trust? What do you do that breaks down trust? What actions can you take today to build more trust with the people you care about?
- **WE'VE ALL BROKEN TRUST FROM TIME TO TIME.** Think about a recent time when you broke someone's trust. Take the following actions to repair trust in your relationship:

- Put your ego aside.
- Take responsibility.
- Meet and talk privately.
- Assess needs.
- Let your actions speak for you.

11

DITCH CRITICISM

Instead of condemning people, let's try to understand them. . . . That's a lot more profitable and intriguing than criticism; and it breeds sympathy, tolerance, and kindness.

—Dale Carnegie

My boss, Scott McCarthy, was almost finished giving me an annual performance review. After providing positive feedback, Scott said, "There is one big thing that we need to discuss, though."

"What's that?" I asked.

"I've worked with a lot of people over a lot of years, and I have to tell you, you are the most defensive person I've ever worked with. If you don't like what you're hearing, you dig in for battle. You've got great potential, but if you don't address this, it's going to limit your career."

I sat stunned in silence. I started to feel angry. I won't lie; it hurt. A lot. "Me? The most defensive person he's ever worked with? Come on, really?" I went through stages of processing and denial, but in the moment, all I had were questions.

I could have let my anger get the best of me. I could have turned away from him and dismissed his advice, which would have hurt our relationship and further proven his point. But instead, I said, "Scott, I appreciate you for telling me this. I'm sorry, but I don't see it. Would you please give me an example so that I can better understand?"

I had only asked for one example, but I got four. And with each one, my boss opened my eyes to what I had missed. This was not criticism—he was genuinely trying to help me. I came to see what he told me as a gift. It was a defining moment in my career because it helped me see what I hadn't been able to see.

Criticism—along with our reactions to it—is the fastest way to ruin a relationship. Dale had a lot to say about this topic. In fact, "Don't criticize, condemn or complain" was his very first principle. "Criticism is futile because it puts a person on the defensive and usually makes him strive to justify himself. Criticism is dangerous, because it wounds a person's precious pride, hurts his sense of importance, and arouses resentment," he wrote. "If you and I want to stir up a resentment tomorrow that may rankle across the decades and endure until death, just let us indulge in a little stinging criticism—no matter how certain we are that it is justified."[1]

John Gottman, a world-renowned psychologist and author, has seen how destructive criticism can be on relationships. Based on his research in clinical settings and thousands of sessions with clients, Gottman has dubbed criticism one of the "four horsemen" of the relationship apocalypse. His research famously predicted whether couples would divorce with a 90 percent accuracy rate, based on four negative behaviors—defensiveness, stonewalling, contempt, and criticism.[2]

The way we approach criticism can either help or hurt our connections with the people we care about. In this chapter, we'll make a distinction between criticism and feedback, give examples of both, and show how choosing kindness can sustain healthy relationships.

Criticism vs. Feedback

Criticism is destructive and judgmental—it harps on a problem without presenting an alternative and focuses only on what is "wrong." Feedback (sometimes called constructive criticism) is actionable and collaborative; it recognizes the issue and then works to find a solution or resolution to move forward, focusing on how to make things "right."

Here are examples that show the difference between the two:

CRITICISM FOCUSES ON WHAT'S WRONG: *Why can't you be on time for once?*
FEEDBACK FOCUSES ON HOW TO IMPROVE: *What can we do to help you be more timely?*

CRITICISM IMPLIES A PERSONAL SHORTCOMING: *You are ignorant and uneducated.*
FEEDBACK FOCUSES ON BEHAVIOR, NOT PERSONALITY: *What do you need to learn that will help you function more effectively in your role?*

CRITICISM DEVALUES THE OTHER PERSON: *I don't think you can handle this.*
FEEDBACK ENCOURAGES THE OTHER PERSON: *Why don't we figure out how to do this together?*

Criticism pushes the other person away, while feedback fosters connection. Criticism is about the person; feedback is about solutions. Feedback is delivered with the intent to help, not tear down.

How to Handle Criticism

Let's agree that it doesn't feel good to be criticized—for someone to tell us we're wrong, that we made a mistake, or that we didn't do a good job on a project—especially when we don't agree. People criticize in different ways. Some come with open hostility ("I can't believe you did that.

What is the matter with you?"); others are more tactful ("I'm sure you had a reason for doing that."); others are passive-aggressive ("Well, if you hadn't done that, maybe we wouldn't be in this situation."). Even if you did do something wrong, what is your first instinct in any of these situations?

If you're like most people, me included, your natural response when criticized is to get defensive and ready for a fight. "What?! I worked hard on that. How can you say that I didn't do well?!" we might say. We'd do anything to prove that what we're being told isn't true. We explain, defend, argue, and deny.

When we're feeling defensive and hurt, we can make the mistake of giving these experiences more weight than they deserve. Although we can't keep people from criticizing us, we can decide whether and how we will let their words affect us. While it's necessary to stay open to hearing fair feedback that can help us, we also need to filter out the unfair judgment from people who don't deserve our time or emotional energy. When you hear criticism, ask yourself two questions:

1.   Is this criticism coming from someone I trust and respect?
2.   Is the criticism fair or unfair?

The first question is pretty straightforward. Do I trust and respect this person—yes or no? If the answer is yes, then I'm open to the comment, and I'll go to the second question. If the answer is no, I choose to ignore it. There are too many unhappy people in the world to worry about what they have to say. If you don't believe me, just spend a few minutes looking at comments on any given social media site.

The second question is harder to answer because receiving criticism can be the emotional equivalent of getting punched. When someone hits us, our normal immediate reaction is to go into fight-or-flight mode, and our judgment becomes clouded with emotion. The same can be true when we are criticized. So how can we reasonably ask ourselves if the criticism is "fair or unfair" if we're upset or hurt? First, we need to keep calm and talk ourselves off the ledge. We must take ourselves out of the equation so that we can consider the criticism more objectively.

About a year after I became Dale Carnegie's CEO, we conducted a 360-degree assessment for me and our executive team. In these surveys, people you work closely with are asked a series of questions, anonymously, about you. In this case, my direct reports were asked to rate me. When I received my report, I was pleased with most of what I saw, but I was a bit upset to see comments saying that I could be more decisive. "What? I come into this organization, listen to my team, ask for their opinions, and try to work together, and then I get criticized for not making decisions more quickly? They want me to make decisions faster? Fine. I can do that. I'll just tell them what to do next time!" It was then that my better judgment kicked in. "Hey, chill out. I like, trust, and respect these people, and they've always been honest with me before. Maybe there's something here I should consider."

I scheduled a meeting with my direct reports to get more clarity. "First, I want to thank you all for your feedback in my 360. I know the easy route with a survey like this is for you to hold back on your true opinion, and I can see you didn't. I appreciate that. I really need to depend on you to tell me the truth. I care about each of you and our organization, and my goal is to continue to get better, so I'd love to dig deeper regarding a couple of suggestions in my report. I promise, I won't be upset. I really just want to understand." Tension in the room began to ease, crossed arms relaxed, and people raised their eyes. One exec spoke up: "I really appreciate that you are collaborative and want us involved in making hard decisions. That's a good thing. It's just that sometimes, I feel that once we all contribute, you could make the call faster. We don't need to all agree." Others nodded and began to speak up. As I listened, I realized they were right. I was trying to build consensus, maybe more than I needed to. That meant more time in meetings, when everyone was already burdened with heavy workloads. In the end,

I thanked everyone sincerely, and I worked hard to make key decisions more quickly and clearly. My team's coaching made me become a more effective and decisive leader.

Callen Schaub is an artist based in Montreal, Canada, who regularly gets trolled for his art. The bright, rainbow-colored, eye-catching paintings he creates garner thousands of comments, with more than a few people saying, "This is fake art," or "Anyone could do this." He's even received messages that say, "Shame on u for pretend[ing] to be an artist."[3] This might have stopped him from sharing or producing his art, but instead he takes the criticism and makes it art. He's even screen printed several critical comments and made them into paintings—and sold them for thousands of dollars. He owns it. He took the hateful words and made them into a social media tag: #fakeart. Despite all the negativity, he has a thriving business and seven hundred thousand followers who uplift him with encouraging comments.

Callen sees a couple of options for dealing with "haters, trolls, and negativity." First, ignore them, and if needed, block or delete them. "This is a fine option if you don't want to spend, or can't expend, the emotional energy to deal with the hate," he says. "But you should also know that hate doesn't go away just because it's not talked about." The second option is to show them love. "We are all going through something and someone spouting negativity is (often subconsciously) projecting and they are in need of help, compassion, kindness, and empathy," he says.[4]

One way to assess whether you should take criticism to heart is to assess someone's motives. Did it feel like a put-down? Was there anything constructive about it? What do you know about this person, and how have you related to them in the past? If you ask yourself these questions and conclude that their comments were unfair criticism, or that the person was not coming from a good place, dismiss their criticism. Harsh words can gnaw at us, but letting them go helps us avoid getting sidetracked by criticism that has no value.

There are times that we have to be willing to admit that someone may have a perspective that we don't. Even if what they're telling us stings, continue to ask questions to the truth of the matter. When I hear criticism, I take notes and ask questions for more information because I look at it as an opportunity to learn. My goal is to try to sift through what the person said to see if there's any feedback hidden in the criticism. Feedback from a credible source is like having the answers to an exam before you take it. You can take the exam blind, but if someone is giving you the answers, why not take the guidance, especially if it will help you achieve the life you want?

That's why we should consider criticism with an open mind. There may be truth to what someone is saying, even if we don't want to hear it. The challenge is to prevent our emotional reaction or hurt feelings from overriding our desire to learn and improve.

When Michael was in college, he had a good friend named Henry who was one year ahead of him. After Henry graduated, Michael convinced him to consider working for Dale Carnegie. Henry went to work in the department of instruction, while Michael worked in the distribution center. At the time, the company didn't have a continuous inventory system on computers, so Michael wrote a program to meet his needs in the distribution center. Michael thought Henry might want to use it, too, so Michael shared it with him.

"To my surprise, Henry criticized the program," Michael said. "He thought it should be done a different way, a way that would be better for him. I felt myself getting frustrated because I was proud of what I had achieved in a short time. My emotions got the better of me, and I emailed Henry and said, 'Henry, I wrote this for me. Not for you.'"

Henry barely talked to Michael the rest of the time he was at the company. "For a while, I lost a great friend. While we've reconnected, we do not have the friendship we once had," Michael said. Michael has a lot of regret about that incident. If he could do it over again, Michael would say, "Thank you so much for the feedback, Henry. Let me see if I can help you out by making some changes to this for you." In the grand scheme of life, it was a small interaction that had a huge impact on their relationship.

Sometimes, we don't realize we're the ones being critical until after the fact. Zach Harris was very close to his first boss, Mark, who hired Zach for a job at his hotel franchise. As Zach's role grew and he moved to different positions in the company, he and Mark remained friends and had a good relationship. When the franchise they worked for was acquired, Mark left for a different organization. Zach worried about losing his job, and he and Mark talked about a potential role for Zach at Mark's new company. Zach was thrilled. He felt like Mark had promised him the opportunity. But for some reason, Mark went radio silent. After some time, Zach heard through the grapevine that Mark had hired one of Zach's colleagues for the role Zach thought he would be getting.

Zach felt betrayed, sad, and angry about how Mark handled things. Zach started to speculate, making up all kinds of stories in his mind about why this might have happened, but the one thing he didn't do was reach out to Mark directly. After some months, Zach finally called Mark and told him he didn't like how things had turned out.

"Mark, I felt like you promised me an opportunity and then reneged on it for no apparent reason. Why did you do that?" he asked. Zach had just read a book about being open and honest to help set his professional mindset, and he was applying its lessons to the conversation. Zach pressed Mark to find out why his colleague got the job instead of him. "I thought Mark would appreciate my honesty and my being direct. Instead of being open with me, Mark took what I was saying as an attack. He shut down, offering no apology or real explanation. It was a very cold conversation." How did Mark respond? Simply by saying, "Zach, that's just how things work out sometimes." Even though his tone was cordial, Mark quickly ended the conversation. They didn't speak again for over a year.

Afterward, Zach reflected on the discussion. He thought being direct would help the relationship, but it did the opposite. In this instance a softer, more thoughtful approach would have saved that relationship. Zach's disappointment, emotion, and frustration came through during the conversation. Meanwhile, Mark felt he didn't "have to take this from anyone."

Now, what might have happened if Zach had handled this situation differently? What if he had controlled his emotions and started in a more friendly way? Zach might have said, "Mark, you and I have been friends for a long time. You're someone I care about and respect. When we spoke about the role at your new company, I had thought I was getting it, and I was surprised to find out I hadn't. Would you please walk me through what happened?" Mark might have been more receptive to that type of approach, and Zach might have learned what had really happened. This just goes to show that criticism never works.

How to Give Feedback

One of the things I struggled with for many years in my career was giving other people direct feedback. I'd worry about how my words would be taken, about hurting their feelings, about the person being defensive or angry, about getting into an argument that could impact how we worked together. For too long, I'd tiptoe around the real issue, highlighting positives while being general around hard stuff. But through hundreds of interactions with people, I've come to realize that especially in business, I owe people the courtesy of candor. It's my job to help bring out the best in others and to achieve results—and my failing to do that is cowardly, irresponsible, and disrespectful. Plus, I've found most people want to do their best and appreciate insights that will help them grow.

Effectively giving someone feedback comes down to two things: our intention and our words. If you approach someone with the goal of discouraging, demoralizing, or demeaning them, that is criticism— unhelpful and unkind. But if you approach someone with the goal of encouraging, motivating, and supporting them, that is feedback—growth-oriented and empathetic. Sometimes, we are the problem; we can be critical, intentionally or unintentionally. We may not even be aware of how others receive some of our comments. So how do we get better at giving feedback that doesn't shut people down and helps them grow?

First, we have to be sure our intentions and our words are good. Ask yourself why you're giving feedback and what you hope to achieve. Second, consider the words and tone. Go back to the "Criticism vs. Feedback" section above and say those example phrases aloud. You can hear that the words and the tone of voice can easily set someone on edge or at ease. How you communicate should match your intention.

After graduating college, Cameron Mann found a temp job at a manufacturing company. He was eager to show his worth and work hard, but he was the only young person in a warehouse full of people over fifty, so he wasn't quite sure where he fit in with his coworkers. Cameron had a coworker named Paul who was sixty-five and very grouchy. He seemed set in his ways and always had an attitude.

One day, Cameron and Paul were fixing a machine that required a screwdriver. Paul was using a manual screwdriver, and it was taking a long time, so Cameron said, "You might want to use an electric screwdriver." Paul didn't miss a beat. "That's the problem with your generation. You're just lazy," he said. Cameron was a little thrown off because he was trying to help, but he responded reactively by saying, "Or we're just more efficient."

Paul didn't like that one bit. Cameron heard how his words sounded and apologized: "Look, I wasn't trying to say that you were wrong and I was right. I was just suggesting how we could improve our performance."

After that, Cameron talked openly with Paul and looked to him for guidance. He started asking why Paul did it the way he did so that he could understand his point of view. Then, if Cameron saw another solution, he asked, "What if we did it this way?" instead of directly telling Paul to do something else.

Because of this approach, they became friendly, and Cameron learned that they had each made assumptions about the other when Cameron came on the job. Paul eventually came to Cameron asking for ways to improve production output and save time on other areas of the manufacturing line. They started out combative and critical of each other and ended up as friends in a healthy work environment.

TAKE COMMAND

"Don't criticize, condemn or complain" was Dale's first principle for a reason. Nothing damages relationships and trust faster than criticism. When we understand the difference between feedback—which is necessary for learning and growth—and criticism—which is always destructive—we can empower ourselves and others to move through otherwise difficult moments in any relationship.

PRINCIPLE
Be gracious in giving and receiving feedback.

ACTION STEPS

- **THINK OF A TIME WHEN YOU CRITICIZED A FRIEND, OR A FRIEND CRITICIZED YOU.** What was their reaction? What was your reaction? What do you wish you had done differently? How is your relationship now?
- **NOW THINK OF A RELATIONSHIP THAT IS FRUSTRATING YOU.** You might have thought about giving this person a piece of your mind. Write down your criticism and think about what it would be like to hear that directed toward yourself. Now rewrite it as feedback using constructive and helpful language. Share that feedback with the other person. Pay attention to your words, tone, and intention when giving feedback.
- **THINK ABOUT A TIME WHERE YOU FELT CRITICIZED**—maybe at work or on social media. Ask yourself:

- Is this criticism coming from someone I trust and respect? How well do I know this person? How well does this person know me?
- Is the criticism fair or unfair? Do they have any basis for saying what they said?
- Practice letting go of criticism that is unfair or comes from someone who doesn't have your best interest in mind. Practice looking for the lesson in fair criticism.

12

DEAL WITH DIFFICULT PEOPLE

Listen first. Give your opponents a chance to talk. Let them finish. Do not resist, defend or debate. This only raises barriers. Try to build bridges of understanding.

—Dale Carnegie

No matter who you are, where you live, how kind you are (or think you are), or how hard you try, you are going to encounter difficult people. That's life. A relative who nags about your life choices. A colleague who believes he's always right. A co-parent who has a different parenting style than you and refuses to listen to your ideas. A "friend" who makes themselves the victim and demands all your attention and emotional energy. When we confront difficult people, we might feel like throwing up our hands and walking away from the situation. But that rarely works—especially when the people in question are a core part of our world. Instead of walking away, we have to cultivate the ability to deal with difficult people and interactions when they inevitably come up.

What do we do when that happens? Whether we have no choice but to deal with the person or we're up to the challenge of building a better relationship anyway, we have to learn to manage ourselves first. It may surprise you to hear that dealing with difficult people has less to do with them and their behavior and everything to do with the way we think about and approach the interaction. We can't control other people, but we can control how we react.

In this chapter, we're going to cover a four-part process we use when faced with difficult people:

1. Establish healthy boundaries.
2. Communicate your boundaries.
3. Listen.
4. Get a third perspective.

Establish Healthy Boundaries

The key to dealing with frustrating people is to start with yourself. First, do you set boundaries for how people can treat you? Or do others make those decisions for you? Boundaries in this context are "the limits and rules we set for ourselves within relationships." Most of us struggle to understand boundaries—what they are, and how they affect relationships. When we have healthy boundaries, we feel comfortable enough to say no when necessary, but we can still be open and connect with others.

Setting boundaries might seem scary at first, especially if you've been raised to think that saying anything other than yes is confrontational, and no is downright war. Say you're at work, and your supervisor asks you to take on an urgent project, but you already have three other near-term deadlines, and you know you can't take on one more thing . . . but you say yes without communicating your concern. Now what? Your stress increases, and you work yourself to exhaustion, complaining the whole time about the uncaring boss. But did you tell your supervisor your situation?

The truth is, you can't always blame someone for treating you in a way you don't like if you've never set a boundary and told them about it. While we may be afraid to speak up because we don't want to lose our job or our relationship, this all boils down to fear. Stating a boundary doesn't mean your loved ones will desert you or that your boss will fire you. It's the beginning of a conversation about how you can work together to create a better relationship. Although that may happen, you decide what you will allow or not in your life. Remember when we talked in Chapter 1, "Choose Your Thoughts," about the things we tell ourselves? Fear of an anticipated outcome often comes from a false story that we create in our heads. Look at the situation as objectively as you can, and hold your boundary as you go into these conversations.

Stay-at-home mom Carmen Medina called her older sister Alicia once a week because they lived fifteen hundred miles away from each other. Every time they talked, Alicia criticized Carmen's son and daughter-in-law, Daniel and Isabel, lecturing her about Daniel and Isabel's relationship, the way they raised their child, and the way they practiced their faith. Alicia was very devout in her faith, but Daniel and Isabel were not. She was very concerned for their spiritual well-being and constantly pressured Carmen to "talk with them" and try to make them "shape up." Carmen didn't have a problem with the way Daniel and Isabel lived their lives, and she didn't want Alicia interfering with their young family. "I didn't want to hear it anymore, but I also didn't want to lose my relationship with my sister," Carmen said.

After months of this, Carmen had had enough. "I thought about what I was willing to talk about and what was off-limits, and then I decided to tell Alicia," Carmen said. "At first, I was afraid, but I went ahead anyway. I told her that I still wanted to maintain my relationship with her, but I wouldn't discuss Daniel and Isabel anymore," she said. Carmen told Alicia that her words were hurtful and unhelpful, making Daniel and Isabel an off-limits topic. "It was hard at first. She didn't totally understand, and she was kind of defensive about it—but I didn't need her to 'get it.' I just needed her to respect my wishes, and she did," Carmen said. Carmen continued to treat her sister like family—nothing else in their relationship changed except the boundary she had set.

As Carmen's story shows, being in a relationship doesn't mean we have to let people walk all over us, *and* it's possible to have boundaries and still show empathy toward others. Setting and enforcing healthy boundaries with the people in our lives helps us build and preserve strong relationships.

Understanding your boundaries takes time. Most of us can't define our boundaries in the abstract—usually, you'll find yourself having to think about them in reaction to an event or situation. Clinical psychologist Britney Blair, PsyD, says that the most important part of establishing boundaries is understanding what they are. "The first step in setting healthy boundaries is to recognize what you want and need and work backwards from there."[1] When tough situations arise, take the time to set boundaries for what is acceptable to you.

Communicate Your Boundaries

You can define your boundaries, but if you don't communicate them, they're worthless. Negative feelings fester when we stop talking with those around us to avoid an argument. Even though it may feel easier to avoid the situation, sharing our needs is the first step to having them met.

It comes down to delivery. We could say something kindly or coldly, and even if we use the exact same words, it's the way we say it that will have the strongest effect on the other person. Michael once had to negotiate with Bill, a salesperson who had previously worked in Michael's company. Bill's father had worked at the company, too, and when he passed away, Michael had to discuss the transition with Bill. Even before this difficult situation, Bill had been hard to work with. In every single previous conversation, Bill was nasty and immature, leaving Michael with the impression that he was a jerk. He wasn't looking forward to it, but Michael knew this negotiation was very important. He thought about what he would and would not tolerate and felt strongly that he wasn't going to let Bill walk all over him. "As we began the conversation, I told Bill that if his voice got loud, I would give him one warning. And if he couldn't bring himself to speak to me at a normal level, then the conversation would be over." Even though Michael didn't like Bill, he shared his boundary with kindness and clarity.

At one point during the meeting, Bill raised his voice. "Bill," Michael said calmly while keeping his composure, "that's your first and only warning. I'm not going to remain in this meeting if you're going to raise your voice. I would like to stay and discuss things and I hope you would, too." Bill looked at Michael, took a breath, and got himself back under control. Because Michael took time to set and communicate his boundaries with Bill, he managed to save himself the headache of an argument, and he successfully negotiated the deal.

Inevitably, your boundaries will be tested, and not everyone will be receptive to your boundaries, but Dr. Michael Kinsey—clinical psychologist and founder of Mindsplain—advises people to use the broken record approach. "The hardest boundaries to set are ones that must be established in relationships where the word 'no' is implicitly treated as taboo. . . . Set the boundary politely and tactfully in the way you ordinarily would. If you're feeling generous, depending on how [the other person reacts] to the boundary, remind them that you already responded and would appreciate that they respect your wishes." For extreme cases of pushback, Dr. Kinsey said, "If a firmer approach is necessary, simply state, 'No.' Say 'no' again. Repeat 'no' once more. Continue saying 'no' confidently, unapologetically, and without hesitation until the pestering stops. If the pestering never stops, exit the conversation."[2]

Learn to Listen

Think about asking questions to get a better understanding of the other person's point of view or why they're acting the way they are. Part of listening well is listening objectively, without allowing our own feelings and reactions to stop us from hearing the other person's perspective. This is no easy skill.

Priya Wilson always drove her blind father-in-law, Derek, to his dentist and doctor appointments. One morning, they were in the car when they started talking about their shared interest—Priya's husband, Austin. Austin and Derek didn't have a great relationship because they had very different perspectives on the way Derek had raised Austin. Derek said to Priya, "I don't know why Austin blew up at me the other night." At their weekly dinner, the father and son had been talking about growing up and Austin's childhood when Derek said, "I never really understood why you lied to me so much as a kid. You knew you could talk to me about anything."

Austin was stunned because this sounded like a completely different version of his childhood. He said, "Dad, every time I told you something honestly, you would ground me or spank me or take away something that I liked! I couldn't talk to you about things because it wasn't a safe place for that." Derek was devastated and quietly said, "Well. I'm getting pretty tired. I'm gonna head to bed. You can see yourself out."

Austin left his father's house and told Priya everything when he got home. Priya understood how much hurt Austin was carrying around from his childhood, so to hear Derek say that he had no idea why Austin would "blow up" at him was infuriating to her. She wanted to jump in and defend Austin's case, but she thought, "Okay, but what good will that do? He's obviously upset. He doesn't need more of that right now." So instead of inserting her own perspective, she said, "Yeah, you two seem to see things really differently. What was it like for you raising him alone after your wife died?"

"Austin was fourteen when she passed away. He was just starting to get that itch of independence, and then Amy was hospitalized. She died about two months after that." Derek's voice cracked as he spoke. "I wanted to be there for Austin. But she was my wife. . . . I didn't know what to do. It was just so much all at once. I wanted to keep him safe, and I thought I made myself more accessible to talk to. I guess I was stricter than I thought because I didn't know what else to do," he said.

"I can't even imagine what that was like," Priya said. "It must have been so hard for both of you." Derek agreed that it was. They arrived at the doctor's office, so the conversation ended abruptly, but what could have been an explosive conversation ended in mutual understanding.

Listening before reacting gives space for us to see where the other person is coming from. Carlos Cubia also wanted to create a safe space where people could be honest about their perceptions, even if their opinions were offensive or ignorant. As the senior VP and global chief of diversity at the Walgreens Boots Alliance, Carlos watched in 2020 as other corporations put statements out condemning bigotry and systemic racism after the murder of George Floyd. Some were simply fluffy PR statements. Others were true reflections of the company's and leaders' values. When Carlos looked at his organization, he wanted to make sure they were coming from an authentic place, but he realized that not everyone in the company was on board with the idea of combating racism. Some employees thought racism wasn't real or didn't understand what was happening. This made it all the more important that they address it with genuine and thoughtful care—he wanted people to do the right thing without making them defensive.

Carlos decided that wherever people were emotionally or politically, he wanted to give them space to talk about how they felt without judgment. He thought of Dale's first principle—"Don't criticize, condemn or complain." Because Carlos is a person of color, he noticed that white men came to him to say they weren't racist, but that they hadn't been anti-racist, either. They were asking for help.

"If we're going to create a safe space to have open dialogue and brave conversation, we can't judge people for their thoughts or what they have and have not done over the years," Carlos said. In some circles, those men might have been criticized and condemned, but Carlos saw that they were asking for education and help so they could become ambassadors and allies.

For people to safely share their stories, Carlos felt that he had to listen without judgment. "This country has been very divisive—not only this country, but the world—with the 'us versus them' mentality," Carlos said. "I may never agree with them, but they have the right to feel the way they feel, like you and I have the right to feel the way we feel. I'm not going to condemn you for that," he said. Of course, this doesn't always work—especially when people refuse to cooperate or have an honest conversation. We'll talk more about that in the later section called "When to End the Relationship."

Get a Third Perspective

We all face the challenge of getting out of our own heads. Sometimes, we're not in the best position to determine what's happening between us and someone we're struggling to get along with. It can help to ask another person for their input. Once we vocalize things, we can hear them more clearly. You could talk to a trusted friend, a mentor, a therapist— someone who has your best interests at heart but can also look at the situation from a neutral place. Ask this person what they would do in this situation, or if they think you're overreacting.

Former CEO of PepsiCo Indra Nooyi, widely considered one of the world's most powerful women, once said, "Whatever anybody says or does, assume positive intent. You will be amazed at how your whole approach to a person or problem becomes very different."[3]

Talking to another person can also help us understand when *we're* the difficult person.

At one point in my career, I had a talented employee who managed a large department. Jack prided himself on supporting his team by letting them figure out problems for themselves. "I am not going to baby people. We're all big boys and girls. If you want to grow, you need to face and solve your challenges. The last thing I need is to do someone else's work." He was also blunt. "There's no reason for me to sugarcoat my feedback. I hate when people don't say what they mean. I owe it to people to give them direct, honest feedback. They should be able to handle it, and if not, maybe they need thicker skin," he would say.

The problem is that sometimes we all need a little help, and Jack didn't recognize that—and one day, one of his direct reports, Mei, walked into my office, clearly at a breaking point with Jack. "He is impossible," Mei said. "He expects us to know everything, and anytime we ask for help, he says, 'Just go figure it out.' He doesn't listen." Shortly after this conversation, and partly in response to it, we hired an outside consultant to do an assessment of Jack's department, which included interviewing team members and conducting an anonymous survey. After completing her assessment, the consultant told us morale in the department was abysmal. When Jack saw the results, and when he read the survey comments, he was stunned. "I don't understand. I had no idea people felt this way." At one level, we might say, "Really, Jack? How could you have no idea? Where have you been?" At the same time, we all have blind spots about things we just cannot see on our own without someone telling us. To his credit, Jack took this feedback to heart. We offered to hire a coach to work with him one-on-one, and he readily embraced the idea. Over many months of coaching, Jack built empathy for the people he worked with and learned how to lead with compassion instead of control.

While Jack had never seen himself as the difficult person, many of us are unaware of how others see us. The solution is often third-party feedback—either in the form of an assessment or from a trusted friend or colleague. For years, I've had the practice of asking people with whom I work for help. I might ask a question such as "I really want to continue to become a better leader. What's one thing you think I could do to improve?" If the person says, "I can't think of anything," the next thing I say is "Well, no one is perfect. Certainly not me. There has to be something you think I can do better, even if it's small." Usually, that does the trick. The person might think for a moment and then say, "Well, I guess you could . . ." Then I listen. I don't jump in or interrupt. I keep my mouth shut until they're done speaking. And the first thing that comes out of my mouth after they're done is "Thank you. I greatly appreciate your feedback." I say this even if I disagree or what I've heard is painful. I might ask for clarification (and I'm careful to do this in a non-defensive way) so that I can better understand, or I might say, "Tell me more," but I don't argue. I want to make sure the person feels comfortable sharing feedback moving forward.

If you're dealing with a difficult person, or if you're concerned you might be the difficult person, ask others for help.

When to End the Relationship

There are times when there's nothing you can do—or should do—to fix a relationship. When we find ourselves in a toxic relationship that leaves us emotionally hurt, drained, and feeling down on a regular basis, it's time to reevaluate whether that relationship is worth saving. Dr. Kelly Campbell, professor of psychology at California State University and associate director of the Institute for Child Development and Family Relations, describes a toxic relationship as "one that adversely impacts a person's health and well-being. . . . When they are going well, we are usually doing well. But when they are not going well, our health and happiness will likely be negatively affected."[4] This applies not only to romantic relationships but also friendships, family connections, and workplace relationships.

Toxic relationships cause mental, emotional, and sometimes even physical harm. The most serious warning signs are any type of physical violence, but the hard part is that unhealthy behavior isn't always as obvious as a punch or a slap. Do you find yourself tiptoeing around someone so as not to upset them? Are you investing more in the relationship than they are? If you find yourself unhappy or drained after spending time around this person, if you feel sad, anxious, or angry, or if you don't enjoy anything about spending time with the person, the relationship might not be worth saving. If they constantly undermine you, cut you down, hold you back, or make you feel bad about yourself, this is a sign that the relationship might not be good for you.

It can be hard to end bad relationships, but we have to remember that, as hard as it might be, the cost of not doing it might be even higher. Sometimes "cutting someone off" can be as simple as not initiating contact with them—just don't text them or call them first, and when they finally do reach out, keep it light, and don't commit to spending time with them again. You can also unfollow or unfriend on social media and turn down for a while any social invites where you might see the person. In other words, it doesn't have to be confrontational all the time.

There will be situations that require strong action, however. Trina used to be a sales consultant, and she once worked for a terrible CEO named Roman. He micromanaged his employees, expected everyone to align with his ideas and methods, and fired people for a first infraction. His attitude created a toxic culture within the company. Trina tried to discuss it with him, but when she voiced her concerns, he only threatened to fire her. "The atmosphere was terrible. We were all afraid, all the time. These were not empty threats, either—Roman had fired many other people," she said.

This went on for years, and it didn't matter how many times she communicated her boundaries; Roman trampled right over them. Trina went to great lengths to take a break from her boss—because he didn't respect her time off, he bombarded her with emails and requests while she was on vacation, expecting her to be on call 24/7. "I knew something had to change when I resorted to booking a vacation on a tiny remote island that had no access to the internet, just to be completely out of reach," she said. "It bothered me to be passive-aggressive, but I was at my wits' end and needed some space."

By the time Trina returned, she knew what she had to do. "I thought about how the stress of the situation was eating at me, how it kept me up at night, and how Roman's lack of respect for my personal life was impacting my family. I decided I had had enough," she said. Despite many chances, Roman was clearly not going to make any changes to the way he acted. He was the CEO, though. Saying something meant going to the board of the company. "When you go to the board to report the CEO, you can expect you will not keep your job," Trina said.

Trina went to the board and told them about the toxic culture Roman created and how it was affecting employees. "I fully expected to be fired, but I was stunned when the board investigated and then terminated Roman," she said.

Whether ending the relationship is simple or messy, take the time you need to recover. No matter how close you were or how relieved you are to be out of that dynamic, a loss is still a loss, and it's important to give yourself freedom to process what's happened.

When we try to set boundaries, sometimes the consequences will change the situation in ways we can't expect, for better or for worse. And that's okay. That shouldn't stop us from standing up for what we believe in and doing the right thing. Trina completely let go of her attachment to her job and made peace with the fact that she might lose it. By that point, speaking her mind and enforcing her boundary—even if it meant being fired—was better than any alternative. When we finally reach the decision to do something about a difficult situation, we feel peace no matter which way it goes.

TAKE COMMAND

Sometimes the only way to deal with difficult relationships is to rethink the way we approach them. We have little control over what others do—the only real control we have is over ourselves. Dealing with some of the most difficult conversations and relationships often means getting clear before we enter the conversation about what we are and are not willing to put up with.

PRINCIPLE

**Establish and communicate boundaries—
and know when to walk away.**

ACTION STEPS

Think about a person in your life with whom you have a difficult relationship. Go through the following exercise, and write down your responses:

- **ESTABLISH HEALTHY BOUNDARIES.** What would it feel like to be respected in this relationship? When do you feel disrespected? Get clear on what you will and won't put up with in the relationship.
- **COMMUNICATE YOUR BOUNDARIES.** Boundaries mean nothing unless they're shared. Share your boundaries with the other person as soon as

possible. How can you share your boundaries in a way that is firm but kind?

- **CONSIDER YOUR LISTENING SKILLS.** Think about the last few interactions you've had with this person. How well did you listen? Could you have listened or communicated in a better way? The key to mending this relationship might be found in the way you listen to each other.
- **GET A THIRD PERSPECTIVE.** When all else fails, talk to a third party who can give you a different view of the situation. Who do you trust to talk to about this? Consider talking to someone who knows you well but can look at it from a neutral position. They may offer advice that can help you move forward.

13

SEE THINGS FROM ANOTHER PERSON'S POINT OF VIEW

Remember that other people may be totally wrong. But they don't think so. . . . Try to understand them. Only wise, tolerant, exceptional people can even try to do that.

—Dale Carnegie

Bryan Jablonski Johnson and his friend Adam did everything together in college. They went on trips and spent tons of time together studying for exams, going to professional sporting events, and working out in the gym. Yet over the years, Bryan noticed their friendship grew apart, especially when he began seeing Adam's political posts on Facebook. While Bryan was stunned to see some of these posts, which were the opposite of his beliefs, Bryan kept his views to himself. They commented on each other's nonpolitical posts and avoided sensitive topics.

That habit of avoidance led to a bigger blowup when they finally did talk about politics. One day, Adam shared a post that Bryan felt was incredibly demeaning toward immigrants. Bryan commented on the post and strongly disagreed with his friend's view. Adam responded immediately and attacked Bryan personally. It was as if Adam was unleashing years of pent-up frustration about Bryan's political ideas. Bryan responded harshly, and Adam blocked him. They haven't spoken in years. "I wish I had sent him a private message or called him to get an understanding of why he felt the way he did. I took the approach of 'He has a right to his opinion. I'm going to leave it at that,' but he was doing that, too. We just never communicated." While Bryan and Adam may never have agreed on these issues, they might have been able to understand where the other was coming from.

Why do we struggle so much with understanding another person's perspective? To start with, we are heavily invested in our own views, and we like to feel confident that the way we see the world is the "right" way. When we encounter people and ideas that challenge our perspective, we might feel threatened and uncertain. It can feel like they're attacking us and our self-worth. We might react and go into fight mode before we can truly consider why they think what they do. And we all know from our own experiences where this can lead—usually no place good. At Dale Carnegie, we have developed a tool we call the "innerview" (this is not a typo—think "inner view" vs. "interview") to deepen our connection with others. We use three different sets of questions to get to know one another: **factual questions**, which look at the basic facts of a person's life; **causative questions**, which look at the motives behind some of the factual questions; and **value-based questions**, which help us understand what people hold dear.

Here are a few examples of factual questions we can ask to get to know people. You've likely heard many of them before.

1. Where did you grow up?
2. What do you like to do for fun?
3. What do you do for work?
4. What's your family like?

Factual questions are important, but they only scratch the surface. We've all been asked these kinds of questions and felt bored by our own answers, but they do help us start to build rapport with another person.

The next step is causative questions:

1. How did you like growing up there?
2. How did you get involved in that hobby/what do you like about it?
3. What caused you to go into that profession?
4. What was it like growing up with your family?

You'll notice that none of the causative questions make it easy to give a simple yes or no answer. When we use *how* or *what*, we invite people to take a little time to explain, which helps us get to know them better.

Next, value-based questions help us really get to the heart of another person by helping us hear their beliefs and experiences. These are the kind of questions that people rarely ask:

1. Tell me about a person who had a major impact on your life.
2. If you had to do it over again, what—if anything—would you do differently?
3. As you look back over your life, tell me about a turning point.
4. Tell me about something that you look back on as a high point or a moment of pride.
5. (Michael likes to add this bonus question here.) What does picking that high point reveal about what's important to you?
6. Tell me about a time that was particularly low for you, emotionally. What got you through that low point?
7. What words of wisdom would you give to someone who sought your advice? How would you sum up your personal philosophy in a sentence or two?

When we work with these questions, we inevitably start to build empathy, which is the ability to share and understand the feelings of another person. In his book *Emotional Intelligence*, renowned psychologist and science journalist Daniel Goleman writes, "The root of altruism lies in empathy, the ability to read emotions in others; lacking a sense of another's need or despair, there is no caring. And if there are any two moral stances that our times call for, they are precisely these, self-restraint and compassion."[1] When we look at the world through someone else's eyes, our ability to empathize grows. We can start to see ourselves in that person and understand them in a new way.

Kirsty Tagg's first job was at a children's shoe store in the UK. One day, a woman brought her son into the store, and right away, Kirsty could tell he was not having a good time. He was acting out and on the verge of tears. Because of her own experience, she could tell the boy was neurodivergent and feeling uncomfortable. "I had a brother with autism, and the only way I could connect with him was to be very patient, to see things from his level, and to speak softly. So, when I saw this lad in our store, I said to myself, 'I wonder what he's feeling right now. Maybe he's scared to take his shoes off? Maybe he's uncomfortable being here?'" Kirsty took off her shoes, sat down on the floor next to the boy, and started to talk and play with him. She ignored the looks from all the other customers in the store and even rolled around on the floor like he was. Miraculously, the boy calmed down and began talking quietly with Kirsty. She asked him to try on a pair of shoes, which he said he liked and which his mother happily purchased. She thanked Kirsty profusely and became a loyal customer, always asking for Kirsty.

Kirsty used her own experiences to make the boy more comfortable. She was able to connect with him in a way that would have been impossible without that perspective.

When we don't have shared experiences, we have to make the decision to listen, learn, and try on another person's viewpoint. When we're confronted with friends or colleagues who have different opinions, the first thing to do is to take command of our emotions. Remember, we want to notice the emotion, decide whether the feeling is helping us, and then maybe choose to let it go. Then, we need to assess the situation at hand. Are we assuming positive or negative intent when our positions are challenged? We have to ask ourselves, "Is this person really threatening me just because they have a different opinion?" Let's remove ourselves for a moment from the situation and get curious. Let's be clear about what the person believes—clear enough that we could state that person's position to someone else as if it was our own. Why do they believe it? When we can look at someone else's point of view without judging or being critical of their thoughts and emotions, we can truly connect and understand each other.

Without empathy and perspective, it's easy to find ourselves trying to "perspective-make" instead of "perspective-take." We can go into a conversation with the intention of changing the mind of the other person or making them see how wrong they are, but that will never get us anywhere. If we truly want to empathize with someone else, we must be willing to see their experiences as *they* do, not how we imagine their experience to be. Sometimes, it's the stories we believe that get in the way of truly seeing from another person's perspective.

Have you ever stopped to wonder what stories you have about other people—and how those stories can impact your relationships? Chimamanda Ngozi Adichie, a Nigerian writer and playwright, was an early reader and writer. Because they were the only books available to her, she primarily read British and American children's books about blue-eyed, blond children who played in the snow, ate apples, and talked about the ever-changing weather—activities that were alien to her.

At her impressionable young age, Chimamanda was convinced that books weren't books unless they portrayed foreigners doing things she couldn't personally connect with. When she discovered African books by Chinua Achebe and Camara Laye, her view of stories started to change:

"I realized that people like me, girls with skin the color of chocolate, whose kinky hair could not form ponytails, could also exist in literature."

Years later, when she left Nigeria to attend university in the United States, Chimamanda's American roommate asked how she learned to speak English so well, not knowing that English is Nigeria's official language. Because of her limited understanding of Nigeria, her roommate also assumed Chimamanda didn't know how to use a stove. When she asked Chimamanda if she could hear some of her "tribal music," she was disappointed when Chimamanda played a Mariah Carey song. Her roommate's perception of Africa was one of catastrophe and disaster.

"In her single story, there was no possibility of Africans being similar to her in any way, no possibility of feelings more complex than pity, no possibility of connection as human equals," Chimamanda said. "Show a people as one thing, as only one thing, over and over again, and that is what they become. . . . The single story creates stereotypes, and the problem with stereotypes is not that they are untrue, but that they are incomplete. They make one story become the only story," said Chimamanda.

When we look at other people through our own narrow lens—and fail to truly understand them—we miss out on connecting with those around us. Empathy and connection start with a desire to understand someone else.

When we talk with the people in our lives, we have to overcome the urge to judge them based on our own experiences and beliefs. Dale wrote, "Try to understand them. Only wise, tolerant, exceptional people can even try to do that. There is a reason why the other man thinks and acts as he does. Ferret out that reason—and you have the key to his actions, perhaps to his personality."

Kara Noonan and her best friend of fifteen years found themselves in a tense conversation during the pandemic. Her friend mentioned over the phone that she didn't believe in the COVID-19 vaccine and wasn't going to get it. "I felt personally offended," Kara said. "My mom had been diagnosed with cancer in July of 2020 and was high-risk. I saw how much she had to monitor her entire life to survive. To think that one of my friends could be so selfish to not want to protect her just infuriated me."

Fortunately, Kara did not let her emotions get the best of her. She paused and remembered that this was her best friend, and she wanted to keep their friendship.

Kara told her, "I love you. We're still going to be best friends even if you don't get the vaccine." Although it felt hard, she calmly shared with her friend everything the doctors had told her mom and what kind of risks COVID posed for cancer patients. Kara told her friend how grateful she was for the vaccine because she believed it gave her mom extra protection.

Kara wanted to know more about her friend's opinions. Her friend was pregnant at the time and had young boys. Kara asked her how she would feel if one of her sons was at risk. The question helped clear gaps in understanding. Her friend was afraid because there were no studies showing the safety of vaccines for pregnant women. When Kara learned about her friend's fear, she instantly felt a different level of understanding for her position.

At the end of the conversation, her friend said she would keep an open mind. She said, "I care about your mom's health, and this matters to me."

Kara didn't go into the conversation with the intent to change her friend's mind. She wanted to understand her friend's decision and stay emotionally connected with her. She was clear from the beginning that she didn't want to hurt their friendship. Through their conversation, Kara realized that they were both trying to take care of their families the best way they knew how.

From that experience, Kara learned that before every tough conversation, there had to be a clear goal. "If you're trying to see someone's perspective, you first have to be willing to see them as a human and really try to understand what you could learn from them, as opposed to letting emotions run over the moment," she said. "If we genuinely want to understand each other's perspectives, and there's no expectation of us changing, then we can have a healthy conversation."

TAKE COMMAND

Taking someone else's perspective into consideration is one of the hardest—and most meaningful—things we can do to understand the people in our lives. As hard as it is, it's important to understand that everyone has a different viewpoint, and every frame of reference is limited, even our own. When we learn to see our own perspective honestly and others' empathetically, we can better help people feel seen and understood, which strengthens our relationships.

PRINCIPLE

Try honestly to see things from the other person's point of view.

ACTION STEPS

- **PRACTICE EMPATHY.** Think about what might have led them to think the way they think: What was their day like? How did they grow up? What do you know about their beliefs? What do you know about how they came to those beliefs?
- **USE YOUR PERSONAL EXPERIENCE TO UNDERSTAND OTHERS.** Think about your own life experiences. What do you know about what the other person is going through? Do you have personal experience with a similar situation? Use your lived experience to understand them better.
- **ACTIVELY LISTEN TO UNDERSTAND HOW THEY FEEL.** Sometimes we have to listen

more deeply to get a real sense of what people think. Ask them questions for better understanding, and then repeat back to them what they said to show that you've understood them. If you hear, "You really get it!" you're on the right track.

- **KEEP AN OPEN MIND.** Often, the greatest challenge is stepping outside of your own perspective. Put your own viewpoint aside, and keep an open mind about what others share with you.

PART III

TAKING COMMAND OF YOUR FUTURE

We've done great work to be at this point, having taken command of our thoughts, emotions, and relationships. Now it's time to turn to the impact we want to have on the world. What do we want our lives to be about? What legacy do we want to leave? Our lives are made up of the tiny decisions we make each day, and if we're not intentional about our time, those moments will slip away faster than we think. Getting clear about what matters most to us is the first step toward making a difference in the world.

In the first chapter of Part III, we'll define our values and our purpose and get clear about what drives us. In the second chapter, we'll craft a vision for our future that helps us live our values and shape the world we want to see. While the first two chapters focus on the lives we want to live, the third chapter guides our direction outward, toward the community we want to build. No one accomplishes anything alone—including a lofty vision—so finding a community that shares our vision and values is the next step. Finally, we'll talk about what it means to live a life of meaning and service—to make a difference in the world, no matter how big or small that difference might be.

It's up to each one of us to take responsibility for the world around us—we can't afford to be passive participants. By taking command of our values, purpose, and vision, we'll create the kind of world we want to live in. Let's challenge ourselves to make this a better world for generations to come.

14

LIVE AN INTENTIONAL LIFE

One of the most tragic things I know about human nature is that all of us tend to put off living.

—Dale Carnegie

Daniela Fernandez was born in Ecuador, a place known for its stunning mountains, Amazon rain forest, and the Galapagos Islands. "I spent my childhood surrounded by nature and habitats, and my love for the environment came from that upbringing. Then I moved to Chicago when I was seven. As you can imagine, going from this beautiful, pristine, magnificent ecosystem to flatland in the middle of the United States was heartbreaking. I remember looking outside the window of my plane and seeing the stark difference between what I was used to and what it was like: flatland and some skyscrapers," Daniela said.

One day, when Daniela was walking home from school at the young age of twelve, she saw a picture of a penguin. It was an advertisement for the movie *An Inconvenient Truth*, which was one of the first films to call public attention to climate change. She didn't know the context of the film poster at the time, but she wondered why one of her favorite animals was walking on sand. "That's when my life changed. I saw that movie, and that completely opened my eyes up to the reality of climate change and the climate crisis. I had an epiphany at that moment when

I realized that it would be my responsibility to do something to help protect our planet," she said.

After watching the film, Daniela took environmental science classes, did research, and immersed herself in understanding our changing environment. She joined a student club and took the lead in fundraising to purchase and install solar panels for her high school. Long after she graduated, the solar panels were still in use at the school. Daniela feels a sense of pride and accomplishment knowing that she helped create change at such a young age.

Daniela's drive to change the world continued into college. In her first year at Georgetown University, she was invited to the UN to attend a meeting on the state of the ocean. Daniela was only nineteen years old at the time. She was surrounded by heads of state, foreign ambassadors, and prominent CEOs. She felt wildly out of place as the youngest person in the room.

Despite her discomfort, Daniela took two key realizations from that meeting. First, there was no steady stream of information about the state of the ocean available to her generation—or any other generation, for that matter. (This was back in 2014, before a lot of specific data about climate change was widely available or shared with the public.) The second realization was that every single person who got up and spoke at the podium spoke about the gravity of the situation through terrifying statistics—the amount of plastic in the ocean or the number of dying coral reefs—but no one talked about solutions. Not one person shared a blueprint for what to do or even a sense of hope or possibility that anything could be done.

On the train back from the UN meeting, Daniela's mind was spinning with ideas. She pulled out her notebook and sketched two different circles. One circle represented her generation, the second circle represented the people in power. Then she added a third circle connecting the two circles, which represented what she was about to build: Sustainable Ocean Alliance, or SOA. She decided to be the bridge that connected decision-makers to young people, so they could work together to build solutions for the ocean.

"I realized that I didn't have any of the answers—it was difficult, and I felt uncertain. I didn't know how I was going to pull this off, but I just felt this immense level of responsibility. I had the privilege to be at that meeting at the UN to hear about all this happening to the ocean, to have this experience that not many people get to have. I couldn't simply walk away. I had to make something out of it—something that will benefit not just myself but our planet and other people," Daniela said.

From a young age, Daniela identified and nurtured her purpose—to help our world. She cultivated that interest as a teenager and a young woman, and when she saw an opportunity to act, she didn't hesitate. SOA is now a global organization that helps cultivate and accelerate solutions to protect and sustain the health of the oceans. SOA has created the world's largest network of young ocean leaders—members of SOA under thirty-five who are committed to the Sustainable Development Goal 14 established by the United Nations in 2015 ("Conserve and sustainably use the oceans, seas and marine resources for sustainable development"). These young ocean leaders are present in over 185 countries. Through SOA, Daniela has launched the world's first Oceans Solutions Accelerator, a program designed to help entrepreneurs address the greatest threats to the health of our planet.

Daniela's story is a fantastic example of someone who decided to live an intentional life and to pursue her purpose every day. In fact, her story exemplifies a lot of the ideas we'll discuss in the last third of this book.

The concept of living an intentional life is a powerful idea that far too many of us miss. We go from one thing to the next, day to day, focused on our to-do list. We check off our tasks, and when we look up, years have gone by.

To live an intentional life is to know your *why*—what you want to accomplish and what drives you forward. Have you ever wondered what your purpose is in life? Have you stopped to think about your intentions for your life? Many people don't unless they face a serious crisis in their lives and are forced to consider what their lives are all about.

In our Dale Carnegie Courses, when we begin talking about living an intentional life, our trainers support participants in identifying their *why*—they encourage them to step back and think about the kind of life they want to live, the contribution they want to make, and the things that are important to them. When people go through this exercise, they often leave exhilarated. For the first time, they have a compelling vision for themselves and their futures. Personally, this was my most important takeaway from my first Dale Carnegie Course—it contributed to my leaving the practice of law, going into business, starting an e-learning company, and becoming a more empathetic person.

Developing a vision forces us to think about our lives, both the things we are doing and not doing. As we discussed in Chapter 6, "Move Beyond Regret," research shows that people more often regret the things they didn't do as opposed to the things they did do. Here's one example: When Michael worked for Dale Carnegie, he traveled the world. "Honestly," he says, "I was so consumed with my work that I let my relationships suffer. I'm embarrassed to admit that as I look back. For so many years, I put my work first and my family and friends second. Don't get me wrong, I loved and cared deeply about them. But I was so busy trying to establish myself in my job—and I found my work deeply fulfilling—that I lost sight of what was most important." One day, this truth hit him hard.

Every time Michael traveled, he sent a postcard to his daughter, Nicole, to stay connected. When Nicole was in the first grade, her teacher asked her to bring in a collection of 101 items—pennies, marbles, whatever she wanted to bring to share with the other kids. Michael was home with her while she was preparing for this exercise, so he watched as Nicole took out all the postcards she had received from Michael, threw them on the living room floor, and picked out 101 of her favorite postcards.

"In that moment, I felt sick," he said. "I looked at the enormous pile of postcards. Each one represented the days I was away from my family. I thought to myself, 'What have I missed?' Those were hours and days in my young daughter's life that I will never get back." He'd traveled over one million miles in four years—and missed as many memories with his daughter.

That moment was like a warning shot—it shook Michael to action because he realized he wasn't living the life he intended. "I took a few days to think about how I could work hard and still know my wife and kids," he said. "I always said family was my most treasured value, and I needed to demonstrate that. I had to adjust my life so that my other values, like work and contribution, didn't overpower this one." Change didn't happen overnight, but as soon as Michael saw the imbalance, he became more intentional, reduced his travel, and found ways to spend more quality time with his family.

Too often, we hear about people who have midlife crises. Most of the time, these crises come from a lack of alignment between what we're doing day-to-day and what we envisioned for ourselves. The hard work, then, is to dismantle or rearrange our life to match our intentions in a positive way. We believe that taking the time to define clear values and purpose helps prevent that kind of confusion and heartache, so we'll start by defining your values and then defining your purpose.

Define Your Values

Values are the fundamental beliefs we hold that guide and motivate our goals and actions. We all have values, but many of us have never spent time thinking about or consciously choosing them. We often pick up the values of the people who raised us or the culture we grew up in without really thinking about it. While this is natural, we have to take the time to consider and choose our own values, because they play such an important role in our lives. They guide and direct us to live our purpose and fulfill our vision.

Admiral Michael Mullen is the former chief of naval operations at the US Navy and served as the highest-ranking officer in the US Armed Forces for five years (among many other influential roles). In all his different areas of authority, he has been teaching on values for decades. "When we talk about leadership today—in a world that's pretty confused and hitting us from every single direction—we need a way to make decisions," he said. "We need to create a framework for ourselves that includes our beliefs and values. I've found that when you're in a crisis, if you haven't thought through your values—if you haven't created those guardrails—you're going to make the wrong decisions."

When we think about our values ahead of time, we can rely on them when we get into situations that are hard or confusing. When Mullen took over as the chief of naval operations, he wrote three pages about his core values and beliefs—integrity, accountability, responsibility. He shared this with everyone he worked with directly and told them, "This is a big job, and here's what I stand for. I hold myself accountable to these values," he said.

Do this now: think about your values. More than likely, you already live out your values, even if you've never defined them before. It's okay for this exercise to take a while. You might need days or weeks to get clear on your true values. For this exercise, use whatever tool serves you best in documenting your values—it could be pen and paper, a journal, or a notes app. The key is to make sure you can capture what you discover.

1. **THINK ABOUT YOUR OWN ACTIONS.** What values do you already operate by? Maybe you value honesty and loyalty or family, and that already shows up in your choices.

2. **WHAT EXPERIENCES HAVE YOU HAD THAT SHAPED YOUR VALUES?** How have you acted during some of the hardest challenges of your life? What does that say about your values?

3. **THINK ABOUT THREE PEOPLE YOU ADMIRE.** What values do they embody through their actions? Are those values you want to have in your own life?

4. **WHAT DOES A MEANINGFUL LIFE LOOK LIKE?** What values does it take to get that life?

Write down a list of all the values you come up with. You might have ten to twenty values to start with. Then, walk away from it for a while. Your mind will wander back to it over the next few hours or days, and when you're ready to revisit the list, you'll have some idea of which values mean the most to you.

As you look at the list, think about choosing healthy values. Blogger and best-selling author Mark Manson explained the difference between helpful values and potentially harmful values. Good values are evidence-based, constructive, and controllable. For example, integrity, honesty, curiosity, and respect are all good values. Unhelpful values are emotion-based, destructive, and uncontrollable. Bad values might include money for the sake of appearance or status, excessive partying, or getting the most likes on social media. He writes:

> There's a blurry line between growth and harm. And they often appear as two sides of the same coin. This is why what you value is often not as important as why you value it. If you value martial arts because you enjoy hurting people, then that's a bad value. But if you value it because you are in the military and want to learn to protect yourself and others—that's a good value. Same exercise, different values.[1]

Choose three to five values that represent what matters most to you and write them down. Keep them in a visible place, like your desk or the wallpaper of your phone. These values are your foundation, your guide for any situation you face. When life gets murky, you can look back at your values and remember the person you want to be and the character you want to have.

Define Your Purpose

If values are the foundation, purpose is the thing that inspires and keeps you going. Sometimes purpose can seem like something we find or discover. Other times it can sound like something that's fixed: "This is your purpose! No further questions." Michael and I tend to think of purpose in two ways: purpose with a "small p" and Purpose with a "big P."

In the first case, we may have a purpose based on our current life situation; this kind of purpose is synonymous with objectives and goals. "Small p" purpose can change and grow, just like you change and grow. In high school, your purpose may be to make friends or get good grades. As a young adult, that purpose might change to being successful in your career or living a life that you're proud of. Purpose may be very different for someone just starting out than for someone in their forties, and even more different for someone in their seventies. My purpose now is very different from my purpose when I was in my twenties.

In my younger years, my goal was to be the most successful lawyer I could be and to learn as much as I could. I wanted to make my partners happy and make money in the process. At that time in my life, having "the finer things"—nice clothes, a sporty car, my first house, eating out—was highly important to me, both because I wanted those things and because I believed they would make me look good to others. For the most part, my focus was just on me. After I met my wife and started having kids, my purpose began to change. When I held my first baby in my arms moments after she was born, it was like a switch had been flipped—taking care of this child, providing for her, and teaching her life skills made me rethink my priorities. As her five siblings were born over the next eight years, I was forced to become less selfish and more patient. If I had even tried to maintain my previous level of self-absorption, I would have imploded. I had to think long-term—about legacy and mortality. My purpose with a "small p" changed with every stage of my life.

Michael spent his twenties and thirties working extraordinarily long days, all in the name of proving himself to others—that was his purpose at that time. When he had children, when his mother died, and when Michael grew in his career, his perspective changed. Now that Michael has been retired for many years, he has developed a new purpose: making a difference in his community and serving others.

Purpose with a "big P" is a little different. Here, we're looking for something deeper that may guide us throughout all the stages in our lives. Unlike "small p" purpose, "big P" is far bigger than the goals and objectives we may strive for at different stages of our lives. This kind of purpose is overarching, meaning it can stay constant throughout our lives—though it can change over time, too. Over the last twenty years, I have come to see my Purpose as serving, inspiring, and bringing out the best in others. Embracing this guides me in all I do—as a business leader, father, husband, friend, speaker, writer, etc. This Purpose will continue to direct me, no matter how the things in my life change.

When we're just starting out in our careers, we might feel insecure, and that might show up in the way we think about our purpose. Instead of pursuing our dreams or living according to our values, we might instead choose a career that promises to satisfy our goals with money or accolades to feed that insecure side of us. With age and perspective, I have realized that the pursuit of accolades was a waste of time, even though it's totally normal to want those things. Regarding money—we all need it. The question is: How much, how do we use it, and what are we willing to sacrifice for it? I know too many people who have lost marriages, families, friends, health, and meaning in a quest for material things, recognition, and a perception of security. As I reflect on my Purpose now, I can see how much it has evolved as I have. Don't get me wrong, I still like the "stuff" just like most people do, but I have found greater meaning in service to others.

No matter what culture you come from, you likely associate your Purpose in part with your work—whether that focuses on your personal success (career, education) or the well-being of others (collaboration, service, family). Doing this can lead us to think that if we're in a job that doesn't have an important title or some kind of power tied to it, we're not living our Purpose. Nothing could be further than the truth. For most people, their job is a way to make money and support themselves. The opportunity here, however, is to find joy and meaning in whatever work you do. Your actual job doesn't have to reflect your Purpose, but the way you do it can.

I met a waiter once in São Paulo, Brazil, named Guilherme, who was exceptional—probably the best, most attentive and caring waiter I've ever met. He was friendly and genuinely interested in me; he demonstrated a deep knowledge of the menu, and he made it clear how important it was to him that I had a memorable experience in that restaurant. I told him that at the end of my meal (and I told his manager, too). "Guilherme," I said, "I don't think I've ever had a waitperson care so much about my experience, and I've eaten in some wonderful restaurants. Why? Was it your training? Your values? Why are you so passionate?" His answer surprised me: "My mother drilled into me that life is about service. I want to serve others. I can make their days better. I may only meet them once, but I can give them a memorable and meaningful experience." Keep in mind, this is not someone who had a huge role, title, or responsibility, but he found deep Purpose in his work.

I feel strongly that our work should enrich us not just monetarily, but with meaning. Life is too short to do work that feels meaningless. Whatever job you hold, I encourage you to ask, "What about this job makes me grateful? What unique talents can I bring to this job?"

What do you think your Purpose is? This can be hard to define at first, but the clues are probably scattered throughout your best moments. When you think about your life, when have you felt a sense of fulfillment? In your work or professional life, are there moments that stand out as particularly special? What moments have you been at your best? Think about the people you were serving or working with in those times. What did you like about them? How did they impact the meaning of the experience? When you think about those meaningful moments, did they give you the sense that you had done something to better your or someone else's world? How? Is there something more you would like to do?

In our Dale Carnegie Courses, our participants define their Purpose by creating a mission statement. You can use a mission statement to remind yourself of your Purpose and the life you're working toward. Keep it short. This should be no longer than one to three sentences. A helpful template to use if you're stuck is **"I will [do something] for [someone] by [using the skills I have] to [accomplish a result]."** But it doesn't have to be that formulaic. Check out these examples for inspiration:

- "I will use my gift of public speaking to inspire the people in my home country."
- "I will use my ability to fundraise to support the local nonprofits in my area."
- "My mission is to teach disadvantaged children and equip them with skills to help them succeed."
- "To eradicate food insecurity for the people in my community."
- "To live a life of integrity, love, and compassion."
- "My purpose is to pursue continuous learning and education so that I can be a reliable source of knowledge for my daughter as she grows up."
- "My purpose is to be a source of hope in times of grief and uncertainty by volunteering for international organizations operating in war-torn countries."

- "To use my servant's heart to make the world a better place in any way I can."
- "To be kind to every person I encounter."

As with the previous exercises, write down your mission statement and keep it in a place that you'll see every day—right next to your values.

Purpose comes down to responsibility. A life well-lived often involves some element of service. Janett Liriano, founder of INARU Valley, which supplies premium cacao products from the Dominican Republic through ethical agriculture, grew up in the Caribbean culture of New York City, where helping and supporting your neighbor was the norm, not the exception. "My parents always told me, 'We're all responsible.' We're responsible for each other, we're responsible for the wrong that goes on, we're responsible for our happiness, or for our lack of happiness," Janett said.

Janett has come to realize that if she is not actively attending to her corner of the universe and working to counter harm, then she's participating in it. When she hears about social injustice, she thinks about how she contributes to a society that can commit such violence. In studying the operations of her father's cocoa farm, she learned that 70 percent of global food is produced by smallholder farmers who make below a living wage. This fact stuck with Janett, and she resolved to ensure that those who feed the world never go without—INARU gives farmers a profit share from their crops and makes sure producers are paid fairly and reliably.

"I firmly believe responsibility doesn't have a résumé," she said. "Although I am a college dropout, I am the only woman of color to ever raise more than one million dollars from venture capital—twice. I've appeared twice on a short list of less than one hundred women of color ever to do so. My four sisters and I grew up with immigrant parents who worked multiple jobs to provide us with the best education and opportunity. Seeing them push through all odds gave me the resolve to do so for others."

Through her work, Janett gets to assume responsibility for her part in society, over and over again. "Each of us is capable of creating meaningful shifts, but we squander that power by believing someone else has more ability. Anyone of any background can commit to adding love to the world, but that doesn't mean it's easy. That's why it's called a labor of love. We could all learn from farmers—they toil with love so that someone, somewhere, is nourished from that harvest."

TAKE COMMAND

Depending on the culture we live in, we may value efficiency, service, family, equality, money, time, peace, success, indulgence, or restraint. How often do we assess our values? Did we choose them, or did our family or our community choose them for us? Are we living our life in a certain way because we think we should or because we want to become better people? Your life matters—don't waste it by adopting someone else's values. We have to figure out what matters to us—and hold on to it. If we don't, we may find ourselves filled with regret later in life about the things we didn't do. As Dale said, "Today is life—the only life you are sure of. Make the most of today." Making the most of today starts with defining your values and your Purpose. Ask yourself right now what you truly want out of life, who you want to help, and then commit to going out and doing it.

PRINCIPLE

Cultivate your purpose.

ACTION STEPS

- **THINK ABOUT THE KIND OF PERSON YOU WANT TO BE.** Write this down and make it as clear as you can. What do you want people to say about you at the end of your life? What do you want to accomplish? What kind of relationships do you want to have? What kind of service to the world do you want to provide?

- **DEFINE YOUR VALUES.**
  - Think about your actions.
  - What experiences have you had that shaped your values?
  - Think about three people you admire.
  - What does a meaningful life look like?
  - Write down your ideas and give it time.
  - Choose three to five top values, write them down, and put them where you can see them.
- **DEFINE YOUR PURPOSE.**
  - When have you felt a sense of meaning and fulfillment? What moments have you been at your best? How can you build that sense of meaning and fulfillment into your everyday life?
  - Craft your mission statement and review it every day.

15

DEVELOP A VISION FOR LIFE

Take a chance! All life is a chance. The person who goes farthest is generally the one who is willing to do and dare.

—Dale Carnegie

Once you've clarified your values and your Purpose, it's time to create your vision. If your values are the guardrails keeping you on the right path and your Purpose is the engine that keeps you moving, your vision is the destination.

Xiaohoa Michelle Ching's early experiences led her to value education, equity, and compassion. Her parents immigrated to the US after living in refugee camps in Thailand and Laos, and Xiaohoa moved around a lot to different schools and states. After attending several different elementary schools, Xiaohoa noticed that she was learning things in fifth grade at one school that she had learned in second grade in a different school. She realized that education wasn't the same across the board.

When she moved to Milwaukee to live with her dad, her high school had been neglected and had low expectations for the students. On the first day of school, the principal told the assembly, "One hundred and twenty of you freshmen are going to get aged out of the system if you don't get your act together." Xiaohoa was baffled to hear that on her first day of high school. "There were so many students who had been repeatedly failed throughout their school experience that, at this point, if they didn't make it through their first year and advance to being sophomores, they would just get kicked out of school. They didn't have a chance. There was no talk of college. The message was: this is a holding cell," she said.

Xiaohoa's vision to fight for equity started to take shape. "It was very clear to me that things needed to change, and I began a vibrant activism life. I tried to join the school board. They didn't have a youth school board at the time, so I tried to join the actual school board. Like, 'Let me sit at the table if you're not having these conversations.'" During college, she joined Teach for America to get experience in the classroom and get her master's degree.

"I wanted to fix everything. Every single day, I was trying to figure out what was at the root of so many of the things I was reckoning with as a teacher. There's no job in America, I think, that is harder than being a teacher." As she worked in classrooms, Xiaohoa met child after child who needed emotional support, struggled with behavior issues, or couldn't get by academically—and it all came down to literacy.

Xiaohoa did research every night and found that if a child can't read by the time they're eight, they are four times more likely to drop out of high school. Additionally, if they come from a lower socioeconomic background, they are thirteen times more likely to drop out. "I was heartbroken. I was teaching seven-year-olds who were already at a disadvantage. I had to do something," she said. This was the moment her vision crystallized—she would address the inequities in education by going to the root of the problem: illiteracy. And she did—she teamed up with industry experts and created Literator, a software for teachers that allows them to work one-on-one with children who need help learning to read. Sixty percent of students whose teachers used Literator caught up to their grade reading level by the end of the year. Thousands of students across America are on track to graduate because Xiaohoa said,

"Enough. If I can do one thing, it'll be to make sure you can read and have the life you deserve."

Develop Your Vision

Now it's your turn to develop your vision. Your vision is the way you use your purpose and values to impact the world. With the same journal or app you used for your values and Purpose, walk through the exercise below. As you work, visualize the answers to the questions and write as if you are already where you want to be. If you envision becoming a world-class speaker, you would write, "I am speaking on stages and inspiring people from all over the world." The point is to try on the life you want.

1. **WHAT DO YOU WANT?** This is a deceptively simple question. At the end of your life, what do you want people to say about you? What do you want to have accomplished? What do you want to have experienced? In the previous chapter, you thought about what values it takes to have a "meaningful life," and how that supports your Purpose. What does the tangible result of those things look like?

2. **WHAT ARE YOUR SKILLS AND INTERESTS, AND HOW CAN THEY HELP YOU ACHIEVE WHAT YOU WANT?** What are you good at? If you feel stuck figuring this out, ask those who know and love to tell you what they think about your talents. What lights you up? Do you like to write or create art? Are you passionate about animal welfare? A good vision will include the activities that make you feel alive.

3. **WHAT ACTIONS WILL YOU HAVE TO TAKE TO ACHIEVE WHAT YOU WANT?** You might start with the big picture items, like "get a master's degree," or "learn how to create a community garden," but then you will need to think about what it takes to get to that point.

4. **WHAT DOES IT LOOK LIKE ON A DAILY BASIS?** In your ideal world, what does your morning, afternoon, and evening look like? Who do you spend it with? Where do you live? What kind of work do you do, and what kind of impact does it have on the people and the world around you?

5. **WHAT DOES THE WORLD NEED, AND HOW ARE YOU UNIQUELY SUITED TO HELP?** There is so much work to be done in the world, and we need to step up and do what we can. Think about your unique skill sets and passions and how you could help those around you. How can you apply your purpose to make an impact?

Be honest with yourself when you define your vision. Sometimes we write down what's important to others as opposed to writing down what truly matters to us. We might decide we "should" do something because it's what our family or society expects of us, or because it's the path we're already on. But if you find yourself saying, "I really should," it's likely that you're writing down someone else's vision and not your own. We have to define success for ourselves; we can't let other people's ideas or expectations of success define what we do in life. You've got to be centered and focused on the things that *you* think are important. Go back to your values and your Purpose over and over again. What matters to *you*? How do *you* want to contribute?

Give yourself the freedom to think and dream big. Years ago, when Tamara Fletcher and her family moved from Jamaica to the United States, they didn't have a lot of money. When she and her three siblings went to the supermarket with their mother, they stared down the candy aisle in awe because they'd never seen anything like it in Jamaica. They didn't enter it, though, because their mom always said, "Don't. Don't walk down that aisle. Don't you dare." Tamara understood what her mother meant: don't tempt yourself because the answer is no. They couldn't afford anything down that aisle. Now, many years later, Tamara still stands at the end of the candy aisle and tells herself that she can't afford anything there.

An amateur private pilot, she was recently at a Hawaiian-themed party at an airplane hangar. People were enjoying the live music, and there were festive decorations everywhere. She loved the theme so much that she turned to her friend Elijah, who also helped plan their pilot club parties, and said, "We need to do this for our party. We need a party as fun as this. I want the hula dancers and everything."

"Tamara, we can't afford this," he said.

"What do you mean we can't afford it? Go over and ask how much the band is. Then ask how much the decorations are. Then ask about the bubble machine. Once you have an amount, then we can decide whether we can afford it or not, whether we need to fundraise or not."

He insisted they could not afford it.

Tamara told him the candy aisle story. As a grown woman with a steady salary, she was still convinced she couldn't afford a $2 candy bar. "You're telling me we can't afford this Hawaiian party because you've already decided that we can't. Can we not 'candy aisle' this?" Elijah smiled, then went and asked.

"We 'candy aisle' a lot of things in life. We say, 'I can't. It won't happen.' We decide we can't do something before we even try," Tamara said. Oftentimes, it's only our beliefs about what's possible that stand in the way. The truth is, there is nothing stopping you from doing just about anything.

When you sit down to create your vision, think as big and lofty as you'd like. There is no one here to correct you or tell you that you can't do something. The only limit here is you. Michael discovered this first-hand when he led a small team early in his career and felt his boss was unreasonably denying his requests for basic resources. Michael came prepared and laid out his ideas: "No one could say no to this request," he thought confidently. So when his boss said no, Michael was so livid he could barely speak.

He returned to his office and slammed the door. But Michael didn't sit and mull over what had happened. Instead, he pulled out a poster-sized flip chart and wrote at the top, "If I Were King, I Would . . ." After ninety minutes of writing his vision of the things he would do to bring the team success, Michael's mental state had changed. He felt excited about his ideas. Most of them didn't even depend on his boss's approval. That day kicked off five years of record growth for Michael's team.

Your vision doesn't have to be perfect right away. Just like the previous exercise, it might take hours, days, or longer to get clear on it. Over time, you might realize that one part of your vision is more important than another. Just like your values and Purpose, you want to keep your vision somewhere you will see it every day.

Know that your vision will likely change. By the time Dr. Stephen Klasko had his first change in vision, he had already delivered two thousand babies as an obstetrician in Allentown, Pennsylvania. "At the time, virtually all ob-gyns were male, and the most commonly performed procedures on women were hysterectomies, followed closely by C-sections," Klasko said. "It was the general consensus in the medical community that, after childbirth, a woman didn't need her uterus anymore."

Stephen was still in his residency as a doctor when he began to question that narrative. Shortly after seeing an older, male ob-gyn lecture at Penn State on the necessity of hysterectomies, he happened to visit a bookstore and looked at the top ten nonfiction bestsellers. Books with titles like *Hysterectomy Hoax* caught his eye—four of the top ten books were about how hysterectomies had ruined women's lives. At that moment, he realized there was a great disconnect between his colleagues and their patients.

After getting his medical degree, his vision had been to be the best ob-gyn he could be. "I recognized early on that helping women deliver their babies is an awesome thing to do," Stephen said. And yet it became clear that one of the central teachings in his profession was actually hurting the people they were supposed to be caring for. At the time, his vision included growing his practice, but after his realization, he now knew that something had to change.

Stephen did some research on the psychological and sexual effects of hysterectomies, which led him to realize that the procedure led to terrible outcomes for patients. "Based on the research, we created a pre-screening questionnaire that would help us determine who would not do well with a hysterectomy," he said. "I felt I wanted to make more of a change and to really affect my industry. As I studied the problem, I realized we really missed the boat on this one—those books were right." He searched out other doctors who were trying different treatment options to avoid hysterectomies and started working with other people who had the same vision and were already doing things to change the industry. He started to see how one person could make a difference and how one small group of dedicated people could change a paradigm. This led him and his business partner to create a business called Spirit of Women that focuses on holistic health.

In some ways, that moment in the bookstore was a defining moment for Stephen. His vision had previously been defined by what he thought was possible. "I now call what I did after that moment the 'no limits' approach: get away from what you think of as possible and look at the art of the impossible," he said.

Stephen has changed his vision and life plan many times since that moment in the bookstore, and he has a list of accomplishments of which anyone would be proud. He was dean of two medical colleges and led three academic health centers, then became the president and CEO of Thomas Jefferson University Hospital. During his time at Jefferson, he led a merger with Philadelphia University and created the first design-thinking curriculum in a medical school.

A vision is directional. It's a North Star, a guide, but there's nothing wrong with changing the vision if something in your life has shifted. If your values have changed, or if you've had an epiphany about the life you want to lead, it's perfectly natural to change the vision to accommodate your clarity. Your vision is designed to help you lead an intentional life, not to weigh you down and keep you committed to something that no longer resonates with you.

Sometimes things happen in life that appear to derail our vision, and we feel as if we've failed. But let's look at how we define failure. Most of us might say it is an inability to meet an expectation, a lack of success, or not taking a required action. That would be a very narrow way to look at it.

Let's say your purpose is to help reform criminal justice. Your vision is to go to law school, but you can't seem to get in. Sometimes the answer is "keep trying," but there are times where we have to acknowledge that some goals might not be part of the overall plan for our life. It might seem like failure. But there are dozens of ways to reform criminal justice without becoming an attorney. Your Purpose is still viable, but your vision for achieving your Purpose needs to change.

When you set out to bring your vision to life, you have to be prepared to pivot. Keep your eye on your Purpose, not just on the goal you want to achieve at the moment. That way, when it's time to change or reassess your vision, you won't find yourself attached to one way of getting there. And remember, your happiness should be a factor in your vision. It's okay to change paths simply because the one you're on no longer makes you happy, and it's okay to decide that your Purpose has changed.

While we encourage you to create a plan for your life sooner rather than later, some of us need time and space to reflect before crafting a vision for ourselves. Miriam Duarte, whom we mentioned in Chapter 10, "Create Trust," floated through life without a defined goal. She had some core values, and she probably could have defined her Purpose, but she wasn't living purposefully. When she was twenty-five years old, she had a near-death experience that caused her to become more intentional with her life. She was living in Portugal at the time and worked at a surf school. One day, she went out to surf at low tide when the waves were breaking faster. After a frustrating day of work at the surf school, she wanted to burn off some steam—like road rage on the beach. She rode two good waves, both huge. Then, as she stood up to take the third wave, she fell and instantly knew something was wrong. When she came back up, blood was in the water, but there were more waves coming, and she had to dive under again and again to avoid the rollers.

Miriam suffered a spinal cord injury and a brain bleed, as well as a concussion. She was in an enormous amount of pain and faced the possibilities of lifelong discomfort and injury. For the next six months, she slept sixteen hours a day and had to move home to Germany to recover.

She couldn't work for a year. For the first time in her life, she had a lot of time to reflect on the choices she'd made. She noticed that her pursuits were never really in sync with what she wanted. She couldn't pinpoint why she made the choices she did. "I knew I had a purpose, but I was either actively avoiding it or didn't know what it was. I let external factors determine my life and the outcomes in my life," she said. She got jobs in countries like Switzerland because she wanted to live there. While she enjoyed her time, it had often led to feeling unfulfilled. She had no vision.

She made a choice to be more intentional. She had only one life, and she had nearly lost it. "I started thinking about what I loved in the past. I loved working with people and facilitating trainings when I was recruiting, which I'd done in an internship," she said. Miriam created a vision for herself that included working with people and helping them transform. "I became a trainer. I've been doing it for five and a half years now. It's the first job I really love doing, and it's the only job I've kept doing for longer than a year," she said. Miriam's vision helps her serve other people, which fulfills her. Miriam took time to reflect, determined her Purpose, created a vision for herself, and put it into action.

Sharing Your Vision with Others

In the late 1990s, I had transitioned from being a practicing lawyer to working as a development director for a top real-estate company. I had joined as part of a fast-track executive training program, had been promoted twice in two years, and truly loved my job and the people with whom I worked. Still, in the back of my mind, I had a vision of starting my own e-learning company. I decided to write a business plan outlining my idea, complete with competitive research, financial forecasts, and a go-to-market strategy. For months, I toiled in isolation, telling no one I was doing this. Only my wife, Katie, knew. I thought if people knew what I was even thinking they would say, "You're crazy to consider leaving a terrific job for a startup. Do you know how many companies fail within the first five years? Almost all of them. What's the matter with you? Don't be stupid."

When my plan was done, I decided to take a calculated risk. I told one of my closest friends, Randall Kaplan, about the idea. Randall was someone who always had my back and challenged me to be my best. When I was in law school and received a job offer from a good law firm, Randall said, "You can do better," and encouraged me to turn it down and keep looking. When I decided to leave the practice of law, Randall was a model for me since he had already done that. He shared with me an innovative approach he had used to network with top business leaders—and he introduced me to many of those people, including the chairman of the real-estate company where I eventually worked. Randall was also an extraordinarily successful entrepreneur; he had co-founded an internet company that had one of the most successful initial stock offerings in history when it went public in 1999. At the same time, Randall could be brutally blunt, and I knew if he hated my idea, he would not hesitate to tell me. After walking him through the idea over the phone, I was relieved that Randall was supportive. Don't get me wrong—he challenged me and suggested things I could do to make it better, but when it came to whether I should pursue the idea or not, he said, "We only live once. Why not take a chance? And if you can tighten your business plan, I'll even invest and lead your seed round. My support will definitely help you with other investors. And know this—I believe in you, Joe. I'd support you if you started a ball bearing or toothpick company." I couldn't believe it. I was absolutely blown away. "And," Randall continued, "you need to talk with David Foltyn. He's smart, he's well connected, and if he likes the idea, he can help you." David Foltyn? David was a leading lawyer in Michigan, someone I had met through Randall previously and whom I respected highly, but not someone I knew extremely well at the time. "Randall, I can't tell David. . . . There's no way. What if he thinks this is a stupid idea? I don't want David to think less of me."

"It'll be fine. Just call him. Plus, if David thinks it's a bad idea, it would be better if you found that out now, before you quit your job." I was nervous, but I took David to lunch. "David, I believe one of the biggest problems with training programs is that people go through them, and they don't follow up—they don't use what they've learned like they should. My idea is for an internet-based system that people would use after they take a class. It could be a leadership or sales program, for example, and then they get reminders that would prompt them to use that information in small pieces over time. The goal is to reinforce what people learn in a class so that they can make it habitual. People who take leadership programs will become stronger leaders; people who take sales courses will become more successful salespeople. I think I have an approach that can make that happen."

"I like it," David said. "I've experienced that myself. I think there is a need for this." He then asked a series of questions, which I answered one at a time. "This is great," he said. "I think I can help you." "Wow," I thought. "David Foltyn is going to help me? This is absolutely amazing." And it was. David became an advisor. He did the legal work in forming the company and raising capital. He also became a friend. As

I look back on starting that first company, it would not have happened without Randall and David—and it would not have happened if I had let my fear of talking with others keep me quiet.

After you develop a vision for your life, the next step is to share it with others. No one accomplishes anything alone. We go much farther when we get the support of our friends and loved ones.

Talking about our vision helps it become clearer. The people we share our vision with may have insights that support the idea, or they may even want to help. At the very least, we create a level of accountability when we share our dreams. If someone else knows about your vision, they can hold you to it.

It may feel awkward sharing your dream, like you're opening yourself up to ridicule—and I'm not going to lie, it might do just that—but rarely does anything good come from inaction and fear. Every time you talk to someone about your ideas, it's a risk. You put yourself out there, and it can feel vulnerable. It's uncomfortable, but great accomplishments only happen with the help of other people. Start with people you trust, your partner or your best friend.

The reason sharing our vision feels so vulnerable is that in sharing our dreams, we are asking for help. People think they should be able to do something on their own, that it's a sign of weakness to say they need support. But nothing gets accomplished alone.

Share Your Vision with Enthusiasm

The key to fulfilling your vision and getting others on board with you is *enthusiasm*.

We react to the energy of those around us. When I shared my business idea with Randall Kaplan and David Foltyn, I was excited about the new company, and they picked up on that. When Michael looks back on the day he shared his "If I Were King" ideas with his team, he said, "It was definitely enthusiasm that made the difference. It wasn't just the ideas I shared; it was how I shared them. I watched my team getting excited like I was. It was a lesson that helped me inspire others throughout my career."

So what exactly do we mean by *enthusiasm*?

The word *enthusiasm* comes from the Greek word *entheos*, which means "the god within." The Greeks used this term when they saw people speaking with zeal, as if they were "possessed by a god." They realized each of us has an inner energy that can come to life in a powerful way.

How would you behave if you were sharing your vision as though "possessed by a god"? What would your voice sound like? Your tone? What would your facial expressions look like? How about your posture? Imagine yourself standing in front of an audience, speaking from your heart about what you envision for the world. You look at the audience directly, you smile, your voice is strong and confident, your arms are wide, and everyone listens to you with rapt attention. Our emotional engagement is that electric ingredient that influences others to action.

Work Together to Fulfill the Vision

Michia Rohrssen and his team founded Prodigy, an industry-first software that lets people buy cars from home in just a few minutes instead of wasting hours at the dealerships. Michia is the first to admit that not a single person on his team wakes up feeling passionate about helping car dealerships sell more cars and make more money. He knew that if that were the vision, he would either have no team or a team full of people who only showed up for the paycheck. Michia did not want to create a company whose sole pursuit was money.

"I was at this very fancy, invite-only conference in Silicon Valley where this CEO of a twenty-billion-dollar company was speaking. The CEO said, 'We're at twenty billion now. We need to be at forty billion in two years,'" Michia said. "I walked out of the conference because I thought, 'Who cares if you go from twenty to forty billion? At some point, there needs to be a benefit to society for a business that's growing, other than shareholder return.'"

That was the moment he realized that having a positive impact was paramount. Michia's favorite passage from the Bible is "Where there is no vision, the people perish."[1] He and his team had to create a vision that inspired them every day, or they would fail.

"Early on, my colleagues and I worked really hard to establish a mission that is bigger than making software for car dealerships," Michia said. The team came to a couple of decisions. They decided they were not going to focus on the dealership but on the individual car buyer. Each one of them had experienced a bad car sale or knew someone who had, so they built software that helps the average person buy a car without getting taken advantage of.

They found camaraderie in being a ragtag team going up against the $1.3 trillion auto market.

Michia realized that they had to communicate their vision to the rest of the teammates. The proof that the vision was alive had to show up in their day-to-day actions if everyone was going to get behind it. So they started an initiative. For every car sold through their platform, they donated ten meals to struggling families. They never did PR about it and didn't talk about it outside the company, but it mattered to the team. The entire company was excited about Michia's vision and were eager to work for this cause. They knew that they were making a difference during an especially hard time. In all, they donated an amazing 189,000 meals.

Despite the straightforward purpose for their software, they've managed to create a meaningful vision together, to share that vision with their team, and to make that vision come alive in a way that helps other people.

As we share our vision, it will evolve and grow. Michia didn't sit down and *tell* his team what was going to happen. They worked together to build on Michia's original idea until they had a vision they got excited about. When we get attached to or fall in love with the first idea we have, we may unintentionally close ourselves off from feedback that could really help. If we need other people to help us achieve that vision, then let them contribute. If we can stay open to the ideas and input we get from other people, we can collectively create a vision that excites everyone.

TAKE COMMAND

Our values and our Purpose make up the "why" of our lives, our internal dreams. But without taking action, our values and our Purpose will sit dormant. Our vision makes up the "how"—our external plans to make our dreams a reality. When we feel excitement and possibility, we're far better at helping other people see the potential of our vision, no matter how big or small it is. If we personally create our vision and nurture it, we can have the impact we want.

PRINCIPLE

Commit to nurturing and sharing your vision.

ACTION STEPS

- **WRITE DOWN THE FOLLOWING AND GET AS DESCRIPTIVE AS YOU CAN:**
  - What do you want?
  - What are your skills and interests, and how can they help you achieve what you want?
  - What actions will you have to take to achieve what you want?
  - What does your vision look like on a daily basis?
  - What does the world need, and how are you uniquely suited to help?
- **NOW SET THAT VISION ASIDE AND WRITE DOWN A SECOND VISION.** Make it bigger than the first one. Change the details up. Maybe this one plays

out the other ideas for your life that don't seem to fit into the main vision.

- **THEN, WRITE DOWN A THIRD VISION.** This vision should be bigger than the previous two, even if it starts to feel impossible or out of reach. Truly let it go—write down what comes to you, no matter how hard to imagine it is. Don't limit yourself to what you or others think is possible—dream as big as you want.
- **COMPARE THE VISIONS.** What do you notice? When you walk through the third vision, you might notice that you were forced to get more creative than in the previous two. What do you like about each of the visions? What surprised you? What excites you?
- **CHOOSE THE MOST INSPIRING PIECES FROM THE THREE VISIONS** and integrate them into a cohesive picture that helps you pursue your values, embrace your Purpose, and have a positive impact on the world.
- **ENTHUSIASTICALLY SHARE YOUR VISION WITH OTHERS FOR CLARITY AND ACCOUNTABILITY.** Practice saying it out loud at least three times over the next two weeks. Notice how people react—don't change it because of what they say, but reevaluate how you share it so they can see the vision, too. Refine your vision as you go.
- **WORK TOGETHER TO FULFILL THE VISION.** Find other people who have the same or similar visions as you and create ways to make those visions a reality.

16

BUILD YOUR COMMUNITY

If you do something for someone else, never remember. If someone
does something for you, never forget.

—Dale Carnegie

What do you think of when you hear the word *networking*? As we did the
research for this book, most people we talked to didn't have a positive
view of the term. The word conjures images of a room full of people ea-
gerly handing out business cards, looking around for someone who can
help them, not thinking about anyone but themselves, and caring little
about making genuine connections. Or it might remind you of all the
LinkedIn messages you've received from strangers who ask to "connect"
and then try to sell you something. That kind of networking can appear
self-seeking—and it is. In his best-selling book about networking, *Never
Eat Alone*, author Keith Ferrazzi writes that the reason we dislike networking is because we imagine the "Networking Jerk":

He is the man or she is the woman with a martini in one hand, business cards in the other, and a rehearsed elevator pitch always at the
ready. He or she is a schmooze artist, eyes darting at every event in
a constant search for a bigger fish to fry. He or she is the insincere,
ruthlessly ambitious glad-hander you don't want to become.

We've all met this person, and none of us want to *be* this person. So we avoid networking because we assume this is how we'll come off.

Recall Chapter 9, "Get Connected," about the importance of relationships. So much of life is about connecting with others in a meaningful way. By working with other people, we help them achieve their goals, and they help us achieve our goals. When interests, values, and vision combine, communities form around a central purpose. In a community of people who support one another, everyone can create forward momentum for their life vision.

Building a community is about finding people who share a purpose. For us, community means intentionally building relationships with people that *foster mutual growth*. Relationship building is a two-way street. We don't enter a conversation with someone we've just met wondering what they can do for us. Instead, we think about what we can do to support them.

You might be thinking, "Why do I need to have a community? I don't like meeting people. I don't want to go new places. I'm not comfortable with it." The truth is, we can talk all day long about how to build a community, but if we don't understand *why* it's important, then the *how* is useless. So, why is having a community so valuable?

People think asking for help is bad because they want to "do it on their own." When Michael's daughter, Nicole, was in her early twenties, she refused to let anyone help her. Nicole went to graduate school, got her MBA, and by the end of school, she had developed many strong relationships and had a community of friends who looked out for one another. Her close friend Beth applied for a job at a large consulting company after graduation. However, by the time they reached out, Beth had already taken another job. She still wanted to be helpful, so she told the employer, "My good friend from graduate school, Nicole, is well qualified to do this. I think you should interview her." That's where Michael's daughter works—in the job that her friend had applied to—and she loves it. The important thing to remember is that if Nicole hadn't been qualified, they wouldn't have hired her. But because her friend Beth recommended her, and they liked Beth, Nicole had an opportunity to get the job.

Be Generous with Your Efforts

In my podcast interview with Keith Ferrazzi, he shared the two most important takeaways he's learned about the difference between networking and building genuine relationships. Forming a community is no longer about what you can get from people. "No, it's 'What can I *give*?' What can you do for this person? . . . When you show up, be authentic, be real. . . . Start by building empathy and connection. . . . The more interpersonal, the more vulnerable you are, the more vulnerability you get back."

Adam Hammes is a tremendous example of someone who gave their time and efforts generously. Years ago, Adam was delighted to be in a cabin on a beach on Catalina Island with two of his lifelong heroes—Jean-Michel Cousteau, the legendary oceanic explorer, environmentalist, and educator, and Richard Murphy, a marine ecologist whom everyone called "Murph." Cousteau was continuing his father Jacques Cousteau's legacy in scuba and marine science, as well as fighting to protect the oceans. Murph was Cousteau's right-hand man on board their ship and deeply involved in the same fight. Their visions were aligned with Adam's vision of saving the environment.

Adam listened as they told stories about the hands-on educational programs they created to encourage people to live more consciously and sustainably—Ambassadors of the Environment (AOTE). "We focused on teaching kids because they are our future. We also positioned ourselves to serve the kids of decision-makers of the world. But if you don't train the parents, the kids don't have a lot of autonomy to do what they want at home," they said. "We're slowly making change, but we're not making big enough changes."

Adam's interest was piqued. "So, we need environmental education for adults? I've had this idea about targeting young professionals in cities because they really shape the culture. Do you think that would help?" he asked. They told him, "Yes, we do. That would be a great way to make change."

Adam's wheels were turning. He had envisioned building a nonprofit that targeted people who moved to the city for their jobs and wanted to meet new people who had the same interests. He knew what typically worked—music, good beer, entertainment—so he just needed environmental education mixed in. He was in his midtwenties at the time and knew that young professional people enjoyed connecting with one another.

He shared his idea with these two eco-heroes of his, and they told him he should do it. He was a little surprised—he had been planning to keep working for them in another swanky location, maybe Grand Cayman Island, and here they were telling him to go out and make his vision happen elsewhere. "I had someone I really looked up to telling me that it was a good idea. Now what was I supposed to do? Do I pretend that I didn't hear that and continue living my carefree life, or do I do something about it?"

After thinking it over for a few weeks, Adam decided to move back home to Iowa, where he was from, and create this community in Des Moines.

It took him some time to get started—he had to work three part-time jobs to make ends meet while he created the nonprofit, which he called Urban Ambassadors. During his first year as a young professional, he studied the process of launching a nonprofit organization. He attended local events, took trainings, and expanded his network with people he met who had similar interests. He also looked for all the local organizations that were working on sustainability. He noticed there were plenty of small, passionate groups of people trying to make change in the space, but they were all siloed. Some people focused on clean energy, while others focused on green building, water conservation, waste reduction, or sustainable transportation. They were doing great work but weren't working together.

Adam recruited a small yet mighty board of directors and launched a website that mapped all the work being done across the city. Now all these small efforts and organizations were displayed next to one another, forming one large movement in Des Moines of people working toward a common goal—versus lots of small but separate efforts. Adam and his team organized volunteer events called What's Missing Des Moines. People from around the city showed up, and they talked about all of the events and groups working on various categories of sustainability. This led to discussions on what they wished was available and accessible in the city. Those events led to more connections and new collaborative projects. "We project managed and got that missing piece off the ground. People were already interested in helping, and we just showed them where they could spend their time and energy to help," Adam said. "We managed to do a lot of good work with the least amount of duplication possible, which meant all of us who shared the same vision made the greatest impact possible."

Notice that Adam didn't need to start a whole lot of committees, nonprofits, and groups to accomplish his vision. His goal was to amplify the groups already active around him and help them achieve their visions.

Adam was very generous with his community and created connections for himself and for those around him. He used a few basic ideas we should all keep in mind. When you meet people, remember to be warm—a smile and the sound of their name can do a lot to create connection. After you meet with them, be sure to follow up with them. Send them a personal note or token of appreciation for the exchange you had. It's as simple as a Facebook message or an email. Whatever format you decide to send it in, make sure they understand that getting to know them was meaningful to you.

The reason the stereotypical image of a networking event is so widespread is because, at one point in time, it was one of the only ways to meet people. That's no longer the case. The internet has transformed the way we connect to people, groups, and organizations that share our interests. We don't have to suffer through those kinds of events just to meet one person with whom we truly connect.

Reach out to the people you haven't spoken to or seen in a while and ask to have a video call or a coffee date to catch up and hear what they're doing now. In her busy life as a writer, speaker, mother, and marketing executive for a *Fortune* 500 company, Portia Mount, whom we introduced in Chapter 4, "Build Your Confidence," likes to schedule time in her calendar to do this every week. "I like to send an article of interest to someone in my community, or just reach out to someone I haven't talked to in a while and send them a text to say hi. I also love writing handwritten letters. Especially now, people crave authentic connection," Portia said. This is why it's important to remember Dale's advice: smile, and remember that people love hearing their name spoken, and they want to know that they matter.

For Michael, volunteering and serving his city has led to more opportunities than anything else in his life. While volunteering is a time commitment, it's a great way to build your community while doing something that helps other people.

Find a Common Purpose

Eduardo Quintero Cruz learned about the importance of building mutually beneficial relationships from his father. Eduardo was an observant kid and closely watched his dad interact with other people. He was always mesmerized by their conversations. One day, he asked his father why he was so attentive to his clients' and friends' birthdays or their kids'. "Because they're people, and people are important," his father said. It was an obvious answer, but Eduardo learned as he grew up that not everyone thinks that way.

That warm approach to connecting and fostering relationships carries over into Eduardo's adult life. At Google, Eduardo and a few of his friends at work initially created an ERG—an employee resource group—because they wanted to get to know other Latinos within the company. With over a hundred thousand employees, Google is such a large company that it was difficult to get to know one another, and the ERG helped them connect. "At the beginning, the goal was to connect people . . . and that evolved into a massive team and a massive group that not only connects people, but it creates opportunity for people who want to advance their career," Eduardo said.

The group has grown into a community with thousands of members around the world. They hold meetings to collaborate and summits to learn. They provide opportunities for people in lower levels or who are looking for different jobs within the company, specifically supporting Latinos around the country and the world. When Hurricane Maria destroyed parts of Puerto Rico, they sent a group of volunteers to help the recovery effort. For Eduardo, satisfaction has come from watching this group of people turn into a force for good.

Portia Mount sees community as a way of being helpful to other people and takes a relaxed approach to it. "As a quick example, I once found this interesting *HBR* article on being an ally, so I retweeted it on Twitter. It just so happened that one of the authors of the article saw it and commented, asking if I was interested in talking," she said. Portia told them it would be great to talk to them. "When I looked at their website before our conversation, I realized we had a pretty deep connection in our work. It's crazy and yet so common, and it really started a terrific dialogue between us. And it was as simple as sharing their article," she said. "That's the kind of thing that you have to make space for in your life, which is genuine connection and curiosity and the willingness to connect."

It's okay to be selective and focused, especially if you're building community around a shared vision. Not everyone will have similar visions. Negin Azimi, whom we mentioned in Chapter 7, "Deal With Stress," started building her community when she was young. She learned early on not to surround herself with things or spend time on activities that didn't add value to her life. She decided not to follow many people on social media, and she doesn't keep up relationships with people who don't align with her values. "When I was younger, I wanted more friends, but I've learned principles for building genuine relationships, and I don't have time to do that with a lot of people," she said. "So I choose a few people who share my values to have good relationships with."

Create Opportunities for Others

Remember the two-way street of a community. There will be times in life when someone helps you by giving you a place to live or a paying job. Remember to pay that forward to people who might not have the same access to relationships as you do, by looking out for marginalized members of our society.

Moses Mbeseha grew up surrounded by family and community members. He lived with a lot of cousins and extended family, and friends often came and went from their house. "Everything we had growing up, we had to share—not only as a means of making sure that everybody had something, but also as a way of creating friendship and harmony." Moses volunteered for the YMCA in high school, and every Sunday, his family hosted their entire church for brunch after the service. Because his parents traveled a lot for work, Moses had to learn how to ask for help from other people. "Life for me relied on a community of people who were always there. 'You wanna play some soccer? Let's play some soccer. You need a ride? I'll give you a ride. You need to be taught how to do this? I'll teach you how to do it.'" His relationships were mutually beneficial with lots of give-and-take, and everyone was always willing to help.

This mindset didn't end after Moses moved out of his family's home. "I always had people to show me around, so when I got to college, I thought, 'All right, who can I help? What things can I do to give just a little bit more? What resources do I have available to get started?'"

When Moses was in his midtwenties, he cofounded the Conscious Connect with a friend he met at his university. The Conscious Connect provides opportunities for children in low-income areas and fights for children's equity in education, culture, health, and safety. They started by helping transform "book deserts"—areas of America where there is only one book for every three hundred kids—into literary oases through donations of culturally relevant, age-appropriate books written by diverse authors. Since 2015, they've given out more than sixty thousand books across the Greater Miami Valley region in Ohio.

When Moses found out about the lack of parks in which kids could play in Springfield, Ohio, he was dumbfounded. "I'm going to find every avenue it takes to make sure there is a park here in the next two years," he said to himself. Moses says that if you have a passion for something, and you really want to see it happen, look to your immediate community. Making a difference is not necessarily about "changing the world." "Think about the issue going on in your neighborhood, your community, and go address that," he said. "Find the right people. I don't do anything by myself. Any ideas I have in my head, I immediately identify two or three people I want to involve. And then I take the lead on it, and I know they're going to support it as I move forward." By finding people he knows will be good at a certain job or who are passionate about a certain cause, Moses creates opportunities for others to work and serve.

Servant Leadership

There is an aspect of community-building that requires leadership, even if you don't see yourself as a leader. For Michael and me, leaders are people who bring out the best in others and build a community in the process. Your success as a leader is not actually about you at all—it's about what you can do by working with the people around you for the greater good.

People often ask me who I most admire as a leader, and my answer is always the same: Alan Mulally, the former CEO of Boeing and Ford who created positive, "working together" cultures and turned dying companies into thriving ones. The *Seattle Times* called him "Mr. Nice Guy"—they're not wrong about that. I've gotten to know Alan very well over the years, and he is an exceptionally "nice guy." He is also tenacious about results, uncompromising about his values, and intolerant of behavior that undermines people or culture.

Alan saved Boeing Commercial Airplanes from financial collapse after 9/11 and spent the next five years transforming the company into a poster child for collaboration and healthy workplace culture. In 2006, he got a call from Ford Motor Company—they needed his help. At the time, Alan thought that nothing could be in worse shape than a post-9/11 aircraft manufacturer, but he was wrong. Ford was looking bankruptcy in the face, and they needed a miracle.

Executive chairman Bill Ford was vulnerable and honest with Alan about the position that Ford was in—he didn't try to sugarcoat it to make himself look better. Bill put the fate of the company before his ego and asked Alan to take the lead. Alan admired Bill's openness and sense of responsibility and wanted to foster that attitude in the rest of the organization. His two goals for the company's workforce were honesty and accountability. No more secrets—every employee would be involved in the process, no matter their job title. It would take the entire team to dig Ford out of this pit.

Alan spent time carefully observing the company, studied competing car manufacturers, returned to the original values of Henry Ford, and, most importantly, asked questions. Despite having the title of CEO, he knew he didn't have the answers—he needed the input of everyone in the company. "The opposite of humility is arrogance. It's poison because it means you think that you somehow know all the answers, and you're there to tell everyone else what to do," Alan said. "As the leader, there will come a time when you will know fewer details than anybody else. It's so important to ask questions, have an interest, and be curious more than telling them what to do."

Armed with this information, Alan created a detailed game plan and shared the vision with the company. Along the way, the team continued to contribute to the plan, and Alan never stopped communicating with the team and their customers. He was there to fix things, but he was also their cheerleader in chief. Everyone knew that Alan had their back—he fought for the company's success and spoke positively about the transformation in public. Because Alan believed in Ford, the whole company started to believe, soon followed by the country. After only three years of Alan's help, Ford went from near-bankruptcy to a full-year profit of $2.7 billion. Two years later, Ford was the most profitable car manufacturer in the world.

Alan learned that being a good leader means you need to believe in the people around you and learn how to work with them. "The leader sets the tone for the culture. . . . The most important thing I have found is that who you really are as a person is going to have more to do with your leadership effectiveness than anything else you do." For Alan, it goes back to childhood moments around the breakfast table when his mother told him, "If you learn how to work together with people, you can really make a difference on a big scale."

Alan demonstrates the core traits of a great leader—he is reliable, empathetic, aspirational, and constantly learning. He not only achieves remarkable results, but he does it in a way that includes everyone, gets everyone working together as one team, and brings out their best. That's the kind of servant leadership Michael and I embrace.[1]

Who you are as a person—and how you work with the people around you—is far more important than your title. What we've found is that some of the most inspirational leaders—those who have great impact—lead with authenticity and put others first. In over 110 years of teaching leadership, Dale Carnegie Training has seen that people are more willing to be led by those who connect with them on a human level and are true to who they are, morally rooted, and focused on others.

TAKE COMMAND

It takes a community to bring a vision to life. No one works alone—we need other like-minded people around us to help us and to be helped in turn. At Dale Carnegie, we like to say, "People support a world they helped create." When we work together, there is no substitution for the strength and influence of a community that cares for one another and their piece of the world.

PRINCIPLE

Find a common purpose with others.

ACTION STEPS

- **THINK ABOUT THE PEOPLE IN YOUR LIFE NOW.** Who do you know who has similar visions and values? How might you help each other achieve your visions?
- **MAKE A PLAN TO BE GENEROUS WITH YOUR TIME.** How much time can you spend building your and other people's visions?
- **CREATE OPPORTUNITIES FOR OTHERS.** How can you open doors for other people to help them achieve their goals? What introductions can you make today that will potentially change the trajectory of someone's life?
- **PURSUE A COMMUNITY THAT FOSTERS MUTUAL GROWTH.** Think about your

friend group. Are they supportive of your goals? Do they have visions they are pursuing, or are they floating through life? If the latter, do some research to find communities, social groups, or organizations that align with your goals and values. Get involved with people who will support you as you grow and evolve.

17

MAKE A DIFFERENCE IN THE WORLD

The rare individual who unselfishly tries to serve others has an enormous advantage in the world.

—Dale Carnegie

My dad used to say, "Make the most of life. Remember, no one gets out alive." He was right. Every day contains within it the potential for new joy, connection, contribution, and meaning. And with each day that passes, we have fewer days. That's not to be negative or morbid; it's a statement of fact. It reminds us that one day, we will be gone. How do we want to use the time we have? Do we want to leave the world a better place than when we started? What impact do we want to have on the world or the people around us?

Up until this point, we've worked on strengthening our resolve, managing our thoughts and emotions, and building greater courage and resilience. We've also learned how to develop more enduring relationships with others, and we've just started to focus on what it means to live a more intentional life. Everything in this book—every chapter, principle, and idea—has brought us to this very point. Now let's talk about making a true difference in life. Most of us dream of doing just that—of leaving some kind of mark that makes the world better. But to do that, we must first take ownership. *Responsibility* can be such a heavy word, and yet it's difficult to leave a legacy without it.

Juan Pablo Romero Fuentes describes his childhood in Jocotenango, Guatemala, as filled with "secondary pain." His friends grew up surrounded by family members struggling with drug addiction, assault, and gang violence. Gang life was not what Juan's friends dreamed of growing up. They wanted to become soccer players, have money to support their families and friends, and live a good life. But they had few resources to create that life. With no one to keep them safe, the street was their playground.

Juan's family didn't have much, but it was enough to create a stable foundation. His father was a teacher, and his mother was a preacher. They instilled values in their children, and Juan always had someone to care for him and food to eat—something his friends didn't always have.

Juan got into college, but he was quickly overwhelmed with school, struggling in his first semester. One day in his psychology class, his teacher told him to leave because he was asking too many questions. "That was the moment I realized my life was not in this type of school. I said thank you to him because that was the best lesson a university could provide. Before I left, I told him, 'One day, I will build a school where every kid is allowed to ask any questions they want.'"

When Juan returned home, he found purpose. "Many of my friends were in prison or killed by gang violence. Some of them had just disappeared. Seeing how bad it was made me sad," Juan said. He saw children playing in those same old streets, facing the same violence and drug problems. "If no one did anything about the crime, the same thing would happen to the next generation, and the one after that," he said. "I thought, 'We need to protect these kids' lives and make something possible for their futures.'"

Juan did not get lost in his emotions. He let the sadness and anger drive him to inspiration. After giving it some thought, he concluded that this problem was solvable. He knew he had to take responsibility for the situation—even though he hadn't created it—if anything was going to improve.

Juan wanted to help people, but he didn't want to be a part of a rigid school system in which the kids felt so constrained. Juan had an idea: the safest place he had ever been was his house. It was a simple, old house with flowers and orange trees and filled with his parents' love. So one day, he sat his mom and dad down and told him that he wanted to open a school in their house.

"Are you crazy?" they asked.

"We need to make this a safe space for other kids the way you made it a safe space for me. We need to do this for the kids out there who don't have a chance. There won't be any future for these kids if we don't do something for them," Juan said.

He was so passionate about his idea that his parents agreed to let him use their house. "It was the most beautiful act of love that somebody has done for me," Juan said.

At first, the children weren't interested. "I told them that I was going to build a new school. Of course, the kids hated school, so they didn't want to come."

Juan remained confident. After three weeks and no luck, he paused one night to think about what needed to change. "The most important thing that I realized was that what I wanted to offer never worked until I was *quiet*. I decided to ask them what *they* wanted," he said.

The next day, he spoke to a group of children in his neighborhood and said, "There's space here, there's food, and you are welcome. What would you like to do?" They were hungry, so the food caught their interest. Then they asked, "Can we just watch television?" That day, three kids came. The next week, ten came.

Juan learned they needed to cover some basics before education could begin. These young people were struggling to get enough to eat every day, and many didn't have a reliable parent or relative at home to cook them a meal. So Juan taught them life skills, like how to buy food, cook, and wash dishes. They focused on art, which helped the children feel creative and free. They played music, painted, read poetry, and learned break dancing. Then, after feeling a sense of accomplishment and joy, they started education.

After six months, Juan's school was so full they had a volunteer staff, started fundraising, and began the search for a school building that could hold all the students. "It's not always about communicating *your* vision. It's about listening to other people and hearing what they need," Juan said. Over the next eight years, he and his growing staff created a curriculum and grew the school into an organization called El Patojismo, which helps underserved young people gain interpersonal, technical, and academic skills. For his work, Juan was nominated as one of the Top 10 Heroes of 2014 for the annual *CNN Heroes* TV special.

Juan credits the children for inspiring him to act. "Because of those kids saying they were hungry, they were afraid, they were being beaten by their parents, that they live in the streets, that they haven't eaten—all those things broke my heart, not with pity, but with anger. You need to have anger and love together so there's hope that makes you move. They gave me hope because they were bringing their pain to me with the expectation that I could do something to help heal them," he said.

Making the world a better place can start with one simple intention. Juan didn't set out to become a leader and create an organization that would gain international interest. He wanted his life to matter to other people, to have a deep and enduring impact. He set out to make the lives of the children in his neighborhood better by opening his home and giving them food and a safe place to be during the day. But with his dedication, he found an outlet for so many of his talents—his artistry, music, and creative vision, along with his desire to help other people. His work gives him a profound sense of fulfillment and joy, and at the end of his life, he will know that he has made a difference to the people in his community.

What can we do to make our lives matter? In his book *The Second Mountain*, *New York Times* commentator David Brooks talks about the two mountains most of us will face in life. The first mountain is the one that we typically equate with success: you go to school, choose a career, build a family, cultivate an identity, and earn money. "The goals on that first mountain are the normal goals that our culture endorses . . . to be well thought of, to get invited into the right social circles, and to experience personal happiness," he says.

Then, life happens. If we don't practice uplifting thoughts and work with our emotions, we get knocked off the first mountain by experiencing failure or grief over a loved one or the end of an important relationship. We might even fall off the first mountain when we realize that success isn't everything. We may struggle during this time, but if we're lucky, in that battle, we might discover there's a second mountain—one that is far more meaningful. "The second mountain is not the opposite of the first mountain. To climb it doesn't mean rejecting the first mountain," Brooks said. "You don't climb the second mountain the way you climb the first mountain. You conquer your first mountain . . . you are conquered by your second mountain. You surrender to some summons, and you do everything necessary to answer the call and address the problem or injustice that is right in front of you." The second mountain is about losing ourselves in service to those around us.

If we're lucky, and if we live our lives with intention, we can be "second mountain" people. We can live meaningful lives that make our world a better place. When we dedicate our lives to doing good in the world, we find an inner purpose we might not have known about. Although we may worry we don't have what it takes, making a difference and living a life of service to other people helps us create a legacy that lasts far beyond our time on earth—even if we just take small steps to do these things every day. By the time you finish this chapter, we want you to believe that you can make a difference in whatever way is possible for you and to feel the courage to go out and do it.

Too often, people believe they couldn't possibly have a positive effect on the state of the world today. This reminds me of "The Star Thrower" or the "starfish story" by Loren Eiseley. It goes like this: A man walked along the shore after a big storm had passed. The vast beach was littered with starfish as far as the eye could see, stretching in both directions.

In the distance, he noticed a small boy walking along the water's edge. The man could see that the boy was picking up something off the beach and throwing it into the sea. The man said, "Good morning! May I ask what it is that you are doing?"

The young boy looked up and said, "Throwing starfish into the ocean. The tide has washed them up onto the beach and they can't return to the sea by themselves," the youth replied. "When the sun gets high, they will die, unless I throw them back into the water."

The man said, "But there must be tens of thousands of starfish on this beach. I'm afraid you won't really be able to make much of a difference."

The boy picked up a starfish and threw it as far as he could into the ocean. Then he smiled at the man and said, "It made a difference to that one!"

In what ways can each of us be "Star Throwers" for people around us? As friends, coworkers, leaders, parents, citizens? We encounter people every day who need the talent, compassion, and kindness that only you and I can give—and when we don't, that opportunity is missed. Dale says in *How to Win Friends* that he taped the following quote on his mirror so he would see it every day and be spurred to action: "I shall pass this way but once. Any good therefore that I can do, or any kindness that I can show, let me do it now. Let me not defer or neglect it, for I shall not pass this way again." When we look for the opportunities, commit to do our best to improve a given situation, and help where we can, no matter the outcome, we are already contributing to a better world.

Yulkendy Valdez was moved to become a social justice advocate after hearing the news about Alton Sterling, a Black man murdered by police officers in Baton Rouge, Louisiana. She was riding on the train to work during her internship when she heard the news, and she broke down crying. News like that was especially triggering for Yulkendy because she had graduated from the Ferguson, Missouri, school district where another Black man, Michael Brown, had been shot and killed by a police office a few years before. She didn't want to live in a world where racial violence was normal.

Yulkendy was in the middle of an internship with an innovation consulting firm at the time. She was interviewing for a full-time position, and she knew the job would be financially stable if she got it. When she arrived at work after hearing the news about Alton Sterling, however, she was struck by her colleagues' indifference. They were focused on day-to-day tasks—making client presentations, getting noticed, making progress. "Inside, it felt like my world had just fallen apart. It didn't feel right to me," she said.

At first, she wondered what difference she could make. Racism is such a pervasive and systemic problem that she wasn't sure that one person could make an impact. At the same time, Yulkendy felt the weight of expectations. Her family had immigrated to the US from the Dominican Republic, and she thought she needed to get a job immediately after graduating to help support her family. She also wanted to do her part so that her younger brother didn't have anxiety around money like she did.

Yulkendy had a final interview scheduled with the company when an opportunity came to go to LA to meet with educators and activists in the diversity space. Not only was she invited, but she was also sponsored—all she had to do was show up. It was a battle between choosing the first mountain or the second mountain. In the end, she couldn't say no to the second mountain. "Something took over me. Instead of going to the interview, where I was 'supposed' to be, I got on a flight to LA to help build curriculum around social entrepreneurship," she said. The power of her dream overwhelmed the power of her doubts. Although she knew she might disappoint her family, she found her true calling during that trip to LA. She decided to go full-time and create a company that would help young professionals of color and equip corporate leadership with inclusive leadership skills.

"I knew I couldn't wait, and I wanted to use my gifts to do good in the world," she said. She turned down further interviews and didn't apply for a job during her senior year of college. She spent that time nurturing her company, Forefront, and met her business partner. In 2019, she was chosen for the Camelback Ventures Fellowship in 2018 and selected for the *Forbes* 30 Under 30 List for Social Entrepreneurs in 2020. Yulkendy now works at Visible Hands, a pre-seed fund that invests in overlooked founders. She is paying it forward and paving the way for other entrepreneurs.

There are many ways to help—working with a nonprofit on a volunteer or pro bono basis, starting a company with an intention to use your business for good, choosing a career aligned to your values which give you purpose. Maybe you decide to donate a portion of your finances every year to support a cause you care about. Having an impact doesn't require that you act on a grand scale.

My dad was a recovering alcoholic. He was clean and sober fifty-one years. Growing up, he never told me that he was a recovering alcoholic, but two or three times a week he would say he was going to a township meeting when really he was attending Alcoholics Anonymous. I used to think that he was really civically minded. Later in life, I joked with my mom that my dad had initially sparked my interest in politics because I thought everyone must be so politically active. I wasn't mad he had misled me when I was young; as I got older, he explained everything, and I understood how embarrassed he had been about his past. What shocked me was that when my dad died in 2017, person after person at his funeral came up to me and told me how my dad had saved *their* life. Apparently, he was a legend in the local AA group because he had gone over five decades without a drink. He would encourage people who were struggling with alcohol to just get through that day. Even though he was extraordinarily busy during his career, he made time for others—he'd call them to check in, he'd meet them for coffee, he'd give them a supportive word. My dad gave others hope, and I'd guess he never really knew how much impact he had on others. But he was intentional with his life and about helping people who faced the same struggle he did. Just by showing up and being true to who he was, he inspired the people around him.

When Scott Stibitz was diagnosed with Alzheimer's, he felt despair and sadness. He didn't spend a lot of time feeling hopeless, though. Very soon after his diagnosis, he decided that he was going to live life as fully as he could with the time he had left. Scott planned a few trips with his family to places he had lived before, like Barcelona, Spain, and places he had always wanted to see, like Memphis, Tennessee. Those trips meant a lot to him, but it was his volunteer work that mattered most. It was more important than ever to him to help as many people as he could while he still could. Because he had a rare blood type, he donated almost fifty gallons of blood over the span of a few years. He took in animals as a foster caregiver. He bought his favorite books long after he could no longer read and donated them to the library so that others who couldn't afford them could read the latest Jack Reacher novel. He volunteered to help people with Alzheimer's who were further along in the process—taking them to doctor's appointments and helping them care for their houses and pets. He cared for other people for as long as he could—right up until the end, relationships mattered to him more than anything else. Everything he did, he did locally, on a small scale, but he deeply affected dozens of people around him and changed their lives for the better. Even someone at the end of his life, facing one of the hardest challenges we might face, was able to make the choice to live for other people and help them in any way that he could.

Truly impacting people has more to do with being your authentic self than anything else. Each of us can have a meaningful impact on the world when we live genuinely as who we are.

TAKE COMMAND

Each one of us has a responsibility to do what we can to make the world a better place. We strongly believe that life is about using our unique gifts to make a difference and that "To whom much is given, much is required."[1] No matter what values we hold, we should pursue personal growth, empathy, and meaningful contribution to the people around us. Once we have a firm grasp on these things, we're well on our way to taking command of our lives—finding our inner strength, building enduring relationships, and living the life we want.

PRINCIPLE

Make your life matter.

ACTION STEPS

- **WHAT DOES A LIFE OF SERVICE MEAN TO YOU?** What do you envision?
- **THINK ABOUT THE FIRST AND SECOND MOUNTAINS OF LIFE.** What would it mean to you to be a "second mountain" person?
- **THINK ABOUT THE WAYS THAT YOU ARE ALREADY HELPING PEOPLE.** How can you do more of that? What else can you do?
- **LOOK AT YOUR COMMUNITY AND COME UP WITH WAYS THAT YOU CAN HELP.** Make a plan to do that.
- **COMMIT TO DOING YOUR BEST AND DOING WHAT YOU CAN.**

CONCLUSION

Throughout the process of writing this book, Michael and I talked to hundreds of young people. Their stories left us feeling even more hopeful and excited about the future than when we began this venture. The people we interviewed were talented, accomplished, and committed to making the world a better place. We were encouraged to see how they had developed a strong mindset, deep courage, and powerful resilience in the face of adversity. These people truly cared about putting their knowledge into action and improving the lives of people around them, and we hope that their stories motivated you to take command of your life, as they have us.

When you take the pieces of this book that resonate most with you and put them into practice, you, too, will develop the mindset and the skills to make a more meaningful difference in your world. We hope you create a vision for your life, share what you've learned, and encourage others around you to take similar measures. *You* can be a catalyst for unlocking your greatness and the greatness of the people in your life.

The highest aspiration of this book is that it becomes a movement for people who use *Take Command* to foster community and make the world better. This book is part of our personal mission; we view it as a timeless gift to our kids and the generations that follow.

We hope that you reap the benefits of reading *Take Command* and acting on it, that your relationships grow richer, that you have a clearer direction, and that you break free of any mental and emotional constraints that hold you back. I saw that for myself in the process of writing—I've put what we've written into practice, and as a result, I've grown into a stronger person.

At this point you might say, "I want more. How can I keep going and growing? What else can I do?" We have three suggestions:

- **CONSIDER TAKING A DALE CARNEGIE COURSE.** Michael and I would not be writing this book, nor would we have experienced so much richness in our lives, if we hadn't done exactly that. When I completed my first Dale Carnegie Course at twenty-seven, the biggest regret I had was that I hadn't done it sooner. I resolved to have all my children take the program as soon as they were old enough. All six of them have, and the impact has been profound. When you take a Dale Carnegie Course, a highly talented and certified trainer will work with you one-on-one and as part of a group to implement the principles covered in this book. The trainer is committed to your growth, providing a level of personal support and accountability. The Dale Carnegie Course is offered in person or online, around the world, and in thirty-two languages. Our advice: Take the Course. You won't regret it—and it might be one of the most important gifts you ever give yourself. For more information, go to www.dalecarnegie.com.
- **READ DALE'S BOOKS.** We highly encourage you to read Dale's two most popular and enduring books, *How to Win Friends and Influence People* and *How to Stop Worrying and Start Living*. These books are classics, with tens of millions of people having read

them. Doing this will take you deeper into the concepts covered in this book, and you will experience Dale's voice and wisdom firsthand. For more information, go to www.amazon.com or wherever you buy your favorite books.

- **JOIN THE *TAKE COMMAND* COMMUNITY.** We will be providing ongoing content, insights, success stories, and resources to help our readers take command in the months and years ahead. To learn more, visit www.takecommand.com.

Whatever you do, don't let your journey stop here. Keep building, growing, and taking command!

Acknowledgments

First, we want to thank our editorial team at Simon & Schuster, including Priscilla Painton, Emily Simonson, Brittany Adames, and Hana Park. They have pushed and challenged us to think differently and see things we couldn't see. We are forever grateful for their help to make this a better book—and they did it in a very Dale Carnegie way. They've been pleasant, collaborative, collegial, and responsive stewards of the project. It means a lot to us that Simon & Schuster brought the very first Dale Carnegie book to life, and we're so grateful to work with them to continue that tradition. A special note of thanks to Stuart Roberts, who challenged us from the very beginning to think deeply about how to reach our target audience. His advice over the course of the project significantly and dramatically changed our approach.

To Sara Stibitz and Faith Smith-Place, the eminently talented, committed, and responsive collaborators who helped us write this book, you truly did a marvelous job of working with Michael and me to bring our vision for *Take Command* to life. For as hard as we all worked over many months, you made this process an enjoyable one. Thank you for the wonderful conversations, off-the-record stories, and the spirited debates—and for teaching us the difference between "swoopers" and "bashers." We're deeply grateful for you both.

To Donna Dale Carnegie, thank you for your support of this project from the very beginning. You always inspire us with your passion for your father's legacy and your unyielding commitment to it. Your early enthusiasm around the idea of writing *Take Command* to help reach a younger audience with your father's wisdom was critical to us; it meant a lot that you believed in the mission and in our vision.

To Alan Mulally, our friend and mentor, who continually inspires us with his authenticity, integrity, generosity, humility, love, and service. Thanks for being an incredible supporter of Dale and of us.

Special thanks to Brenda Leigh Johnson, who checked our historical facts about Dale; to Chris Caughell, who helped co-lead our advisory council and who coordinated a significant amount of outreach seamlessly; and to Cliff Heckman, for your pleasant persistence in keeping us on track throughout this project, even if it felt like herding cats at times.

To Carnegie Master and VP of Training Ercell Charles, the man we call "The Protector of the Flame"—thank you for keeping the Carnegie spirit alive, and for coming to the table with fresh ideas and energy every time.

To Christine Buscarino, thank you for your listening ear, thoughtful insight, and constant support.

To all of the people who contributed stories: Adam Hammes, Alan Mulally, Alex Schwarzkopf, Ally Love, Andy Zinsmeister, Artis Stevens, Bryan Jablonski Johnson, Callen Schaub, Cameron Mann, Camille Chang Gilmore, Carlos Cubia, Daniela Fernandez, David Barrios, Deborah Ann Mack, Eduardo Quintero Cruz, Janett Liriano, Jenny Xu, Jéssika Santiago, John and Betty Mobbs, Juan Pablo Romero Fuentes, Kara Noonan, Katie Dill, Keith Ferrazzi, Kirsty Tagg, Lea Gabrielle, Luke Maguire Armstrong, Marshall Goldsmith, Michael Mullen, Michia Rohrssen, Miriam Duarte, Moses Mbeseha, Negin Azimi, Nicole Crom, Portia Mount, Ron Carter, Ryan Chen, Stephen Klasko, Tamara Fletcher, Tim Reilly, Wendy Wang, Xiaohoa Michelle Ching, Yesenia Aguirre, Yulkendy Valdez, Yuri Kruman, and all the others who wish to remain anonymous. Even though we weren't able to include all of the stories we received, we're so thankful for every single individual who shared their successes, their failures, their wisdom, and their heart with us. You have inspired us more than you know. Each and every one of you left us excited about the future. We both felt that you were some of the most interesting people we've talked to in our lives, and you left us thinking that you would move mountains and make a real difference in the world. Thank you for vulnerably sharing your experiences. Your authenticity breathed life into this book.

To our absolutely amazing advisory council: Bryan Jablonski Johnson, Cameron Mann, Darrell Pickering, Diana Menendez, Gaweed El Nakeeb, Jéssika Santiago, Joe Gannon, Kara Noonan, Khadidja Guerrab, Kirsty Tagg, Miriam Duarte, Natalie Glaneman, Nicholas McMullen, Tsvetelina Kemalova, and Wendy Wang. You all have been extraordinary. You contributed countless hours on top of already packed schedules. You brought insight that has had a tremendous impact on the principles, structure, and focus of this book. The diversity and perspective you provided have greatly enhanced our ability to deliver this book to a global audience. You model Dale's principles with enthusiasm and genuine care. We are truly grateful for each of you.

To our Dale Carnegie franchisees and their teams, as well as to our Dale Carnegie Training team, thank you for all that you do. You are the ones who work together to deliver Dale's wisdom to people around the world and who keep his dream alive, day in and out. We can't thank you enough for being partners in this vision.

To our shareholders and board of directors, who have been supportive of our efforts to write this book, and who continue to be huge advocates and believers in the brand, thank you for your investment and belief in us.

To all of our customers who trust us to help unlock their greatness and that of their people, you are the reason we do what we do. We are grateful and humbled to share in your journey and to contribute to your success.

From Joe

I would like to thank and recognize my family: my wife, Katie; my children, Abby, Ellie, Maggie, Mary Kate, Thomas, and Johnathan; my mom, Rosalie; and my brother, Brian. I love you all so much and am proud and grateful to call you my family. This book took an incredible amount of time and commitment, and you supported me through it all. I want to acknowledge your sacrifice. It was not lost on me that, for a significant amount of time, you had to put up with an unavailable spouse, father, son, or brother. To my dad, Joe, I miss you greatly but know how proud you are of me and this book. To Mom: you've always been there for me, and I could not have had a more loving and selfless mother. To Katie: as always, your support has been unreal. You've been with me in everything I've done—without guilt, selfishness, or resentment. You've been "all in" every time; I couldn't do what I do without you, and I love you with all my heart.

From Michael

To my wife, Nancy, who has been incredibly supportive and eager for me to take on this project from the very start. Thank you for your generosity; this book took a lot of my time, and you were patient and encouraging through it all. To my daughter, Nicole, thank you for reading early drafts and sharing page after page of thoughts and ideas for the book. Your support has been incredible. To my son, Alex, thank you for your perspectives on how our audience would respond to the ideas and principles in this book. You provided a lot of clarity. Finally, thank you to my parents, Ollie and Rosemary Crom, for a lifetime of providing inspiration and incredible examples of how to live an intentional life.

Notes

Chapter 1: Choose Your Thoughts

1. Marcus Aurelius (Emperor of Rome), *The Meditations of Marcus Aurelius* (Boston: Shambhala, 1993).
2. Amrisha Vaish, Tobias Grossmann, and Amanda Woodward, "Not All Emotions Are Created Equal: The Negativity Bias in Social-Emotional Development," *Psychological Bulletin* 134, no. 3 (May 2008): 383–403. https://doi.org/10.1037/0033-2909.134.3.383.
3. Verywell Mind, "What Is the Negativity Bias?" https://www.verywellmind.com/negative-bias-4589618, accessed June 10, 2022.
4. The Strive Team, "What Are Affirmations & Why Should You Use Them?," *The STRIVE* (blog), August 18, 2021. https://thestrive.co/what-are-affirmations/.

Chapter 2: Condition Your Mind for Success

1. Benjamin Enrique and Blaine McCormick, *Ben Franklin: America's Original Entrepreneur* (Irvine, CA: Entrepreneur Press, 2005).
2. Haruki Murakami, "The Art of Fiction No. 182," interview by John Wray, *Paris Review*, no. 170 (Summer 2004), https://www.theparisreview.org/interviews/2/the-art-of-fiction-no-182-haruki-murakami.
3. "Study Shows a Pre-Game Routine Can Boost an Athlete's Performance," *Medical Xpress*, November 29, 2021. https://medicalxpress.com/news/2021-11-pre-game-routine-boost-athlete.html, accessed June 11, 2022.
4. Carol S. Dweck, *Mindset: The New Psychology of Success* (New York: Ballantine Books, 2008).
5. Guang Zeng, Hanchao Hou, and Kaiping Peng, "Effect of Growth Mindset on School Engagement and Psychological Well-Being of Chinese Primary and Middle School Students: The Mediating Role of Resilience," *Frontiers in Psychology* 7 (2016), https://doi.org/10.3389/fpsyg.2016.01873.

6. James Clear, "How to Build a New Habit: This Is Your Strategy Guide," JamesClear.com, July 18, 2014, https://jamesclear.com/habit-guide.

Chapter 3: Work with Your Emotions

1. Laith Al-Shawaf, Daniel Conroy-Beam, Kelly Asao, and David M. Buss, "Human Emotions: An Evolutionary Psychological Perspective," *Emotion Review* 8, no. 2 (April 2016): 173–86, https://doi.org/10.1177/1754073914565518.
2. Emiliya Zhivotovskaya, "The Many Gifts of Positive Emotions," The Flourishing Center, June 9, 2015, https://theflourishingcenter.com/the-many-gifts-of-positive-emotions/.
3. Nora Marie Raschle et al., "Emotions and the Brain—Or How to Master 'The Force,'" *Frontiers for Young Minds*, September 12, 2016, https://kids.frontiersin.org/articles/10.3389/frym.2016.00016, accessed June 12, 2022.
4. Stamen Design, "The Ekmans' Atlas of Emotion," http://atlasofemotions.org/, accessed June 12, 2022.
5. *Psychology and Counseling News*, "The Science of Emotion: Exploring the Basics of Emotional Psychology," June 27, 2019, https://online.uwa.edu/news/emotional-psychology/.
6. Brené Brown, *Atlas of the Heart: Mapping Meaningful Connection and the Language of Human Experience* (New York: Random House, 2021).
7. Edith Eva Eger, *The Choice: Embrace the Possible*, with Esmé Schwall Weigand (New York: Scribner, 2018).
8. Susan A. David, *Emotional Agility: Get Unstuck, Embrace Change, and Thrive in Work and Life* (New York: Avery, 2016).
9. Bryan E. Robinson, "The 90-Second Rule That Builds Self-Control," *Psychology Today*, accessed June 12, 2022, https://www.psychologytoday.com/ca/blog/the-right-mindset/202004/the-90-second-rule-builds-self-control.

Chapter 4: Build Your Confidence

1. Tara Westover, *Educated: A Memoir* (New York: Random House, 2018).
2. Mihika Agarwal, "Attacked with Acid at Two-Months-Old, Anmol Rodriguez's Story Is One of Thriving, Not Surviving," *Vogue India*, January 9, 2020. https://www.vogue.in/culture-and-living/content/acid-attack-survivor-anmol-rodriguez-social-media-instagram-influencer-model.
3. Kristin Neff, "Why Self-Compassion Trumps Self-Esteem," *Greater Good Magazine*, May 27, 2011, https://greatergood.berkeley.edu/article/item/try_selfcompassion, accessed June 12, 2022.

Chapter 5: Embrace Change

1. Viktor E. Frankl, *Man's Search for Meaning*, translated by Ilse Lasch, with a foreword by Harold S. Kushner and afterword by William J. Winslade (Boston: Beacon Press, 2006).

2. Angela Duckworth, "What Is the Difference between Resilience and Grit?," DukeEthics Virtues & Vocations Reimagining Education series, July 31, 2020, video, 2:17, https://www.youtube.com /watch?v=05XmoKKrj4M.

3. Susan A. David, *Emotional Agility: Get Unstuck, Embrace Change, and Thrive in Work and Life* (New York: Avery, 2016).

Chapter 6: Move Beyond Regret

1. Daniel H. Pink, *The Power of Regret: How Looking Backward Moves Us Forward* (New York: Riverhead, 2022).

Chapter 7: Deal with Stress

1. Cleveland Clinic, "Stress: Signs, Symptoms, Management & Prevention," January 28, 2021, https://my.clevelandclinic.org/health/articles/11874-stress, accessed June 10, 2022.

2. Amanda Barrell, "Stress vs. Anxiety: Differences, Symptoms, and Relief," *MedicalNewsToday*, April 24, 2020, https://www.medicalnewstoday.com/articles /stress-vs-anxiety.

3. Barrell, "Stress vs. Anxiety."

4. Barrell, "Stress vs. Anxiety."

5. Kelly McGonigal, "How to Make Stress Your Friend," TEDGlobal, Edinburgh, September 4, 2013, video, https://www.ted.com/talks/kelly_mcgonigal _how_to_make_stress_your_friend.

6. McGonigal, "How to Make Stress Your Friend."

7. McGonigal, "How to Make Stress Your Friend."

8. Jessica Sager, "You Can Feel Burnout in Your Body—Here Are the 15 Physical Symptoms to Pay Attention to, According to Doctors," *Parade*, March 1, 2022, https://parade.com/1341134/jessicasager/physical-symptoms-burnout/.

9. Alexandra Michel, "Burnout and the Brain," *APS Observer* 29, no. 2 (February 2016), https://www.psychologicalscience.org/observer/burnout-and-the-brain.

10. Stacey Lindsay, "Why You're Still Tired: Dr. Saundra Dalton-Smith on the 7 Types of Rest We All Need," MariaShriver.com, December 20, 2020, https:// mariashriver.com/why-youre-still-tired-dr-saundra-dalton-smith-on-the -7-types-of-rest-we-all-need/.

11. *Healthy Living*, "Get Enough Sleep," MyHealthfinder, https://health.gov /myhealthfinder/healthy-living/mental-health-and-relationships/get -enough-sleep, accessed June 14, 2022.

Chapter 8: Build Resilience and Courage

1. USC staff, "Bina Venkataraman: 'It Takes Courage to Ask: Is It Possible to Do What People Say Is Impossible?'," *USC News*, May 17, 2021, https://news.usc .edu/186442/usc-2021-commencement-speaker-bina-venkataraman/.
2. Dale Carnegie & Associates, Inc., "Developing Resilience in the Workplace," 2020, https://www.dalecarnegie.com/en/resources/developing-a-resilient -workforce-how-organizations-thrive-in-the-face-of-adversity.
3. Lucy Hone, "3 Secrets of Resilient People," TEDxChristchurch, August 2019, video, 16:05, https://www.ted.com/talks/lucy_hone_3_secrets_of_resilient _people.

Chapter 9: Get Connected

1. Dale Carnegie, *How to Win Friends and Influence People* (New Delhi: Srishti Publishers & Distributors, 2020).
2. Liz Mineo, "Good Genes Are Nice but Joy Is Better," *Harvard Gazette*, April 11, 2017, https://news.harvard.edu/gazette/story/2017/04/over-nearly-80-years -harvard-study-has-been-showing-how-to-live-a-healthy-and-happy-life/.
3. Robert Waldinger, "What Makes a Good Life? Lessons from the Longest Study on Happiness," TEDxBeaconStreet, November 2015, video, 12:38, https://www.ted.com/talks/robert_waldinger_what_makes_a_good_life_les sons_from_the_longest_study_on_happiness.
4. Taking Charge of Your Health & Wellbeing, "Why Personal Relationships Are Important," University of Minnesota, https://www.takingcharge.csh.umn .edu/why-personal-relationships-are-important, accessed June 10, 2022.
5. Taking Charge of Your Health & Wellbeing, "Stress Mastery," University of Minnesota, https://www.takingcharge.csh.umn.edu/stress-mastery, accessed June 10, 2022.
6. Taking Charge of Your Health & Wellbeing, "Why Personal Relationships Are Important."
7. Vanessa Van Edwards, "What Makes Someone Charismatic?," LinkedIn, March 9, 2022, https://www.linkedin.com/pulse/what-makes-someone-char ismatic-vanessa-van-edwards/?trk=pulse-article_more-articles_related-con tent-card, accessed June 16, 2022.

8. "How Much of Communication Is Nonverbal?," UT Permian Basin online, November 3, 2020, https://online.utpb.edu/about-us/articles/communication/how-much-of-communication-is-nonverbal.
9. Carnegie, *How to Win Friends and Influence People.*
10. Brené Brown, in "Brene Brown Quotes," BrainyQuote, https://www.brainyquote.com/quotes/brene_brown_553082, accessed June 16, 2022.
11. Catherine Hiley, "How Much of Your Time Is Screen Time?," Uswitch, June 15, 2021, https://www.uswitch.com/mobiles/screentime-report/, accessed June 16, 2022.
12. Jean Twenge, "Teens Have Less Face Time with Their Friends—and Are Lonelier than Ever," *The Conversation*, March 20, 2019, http://theconversation.com/teens-have-less-face-time-with-their-friends-and-are-lonelier-than-ever-113240, accessed June 16, 2022.

Chapter 10: Create Trust

1. Erik H. Erikson, *Childhood and Society* (New York: W. W. Norton & Company, 1993).
2. "Where Trust Is High, Crime and Corruption Are Low," Pew Research Center's Global Attitudes Project, April 15, 2008, https://www.pewresearch.org/global/2008/04/15/where-trust-is-high-crime-and-corruption-are-low/.
3. Arthur Ashe, "Quotes," CMG Worldwide, http://www.cmgww.com/sports/ashe/quotes/.

Chapter 11: Ditch Criticism

1. Carnegie, *How to Win Friends and Influence People.*
2. Ellie Lisitsa, "The Four Horsemen: Criticism, Contempt, Defensiveness, and Stonewalling," The Gottman Institute, April 24, 2013, https://www.gottman.com/blog/the-four-horsemen-recognizing-criticism-contempt-defensiveness-and-stonewalling/.
3. Callen Schaub (@callenschaub), "Shame sh*t different day! Haters as motivators 🤍 😂 Let's keep making the world more colorful no matter what they say 🎨🎨🎨🎨🎨🎨🎨 #fakeart #fakeartmovement," Instagram post, March 29, 2022, https://www.instagram.com/p/CbtAkssL8cz/?hl=en, accessed June 17, 2022.
4. Callen Schaub (@callenschaub), "I don't have this fully worked out but here is a rough draft. Let's work on it together. . . . What tier do you favor, how can we make this system better. May delete later,," Instagram post, August 13, 2021, https://www.instagram.com/p/CSh4fj6FGnl, accessed June 17, 2022.

Chapter 12: Deal with Difficult People

1. Hedy Phillips, "How to More Effectively Set Boundaries, According to Therapists," *POPSUGAR Fitness*, December 22, 2020, https://www.popsugar.com/node/48026080.
2. Phillips, "How to More Effectively Set Boundaries."
3. Indra Nooyi, "The Best Advice I Ever Got," *Fortune*, April 30, 2008, https://archive.fortune.com/galleries/2008/fortune/0804/gallery.bestadvice.fortune/7.html.
4. Kelly Dawson, "How to Leave a Toxic Relationship, According to a Psychologist," *Brides*, updated May 23, 2022, https://www.brides.com/how-to-leave-a-toxic-relationship-5105346, accessed June 18, 2022.

Chapter 13: See Things from Another Person's Point of View

1. Daniel Goleman, *Emotional Intelligence: Why It Can Matter More Than IQ*, 10th anniversary edition (New York: Bantam Books, 2012).

Chapter 14: Live an Intentional Life

1. Mark Manson, "Personal Values: How to Know Who You Really Are," *Mark Manson*, January 22, 2021, https://markmanson.net/personal-values.

Chapter 15: Develop a Vision for Life

1. Proverbs 29:18, King James Version, https://www.biblegateway.com/passage/?search=Proverbs%2029%3A18&version=KJV, accessed June 19, 2022.

Chapter 16: Build Your Community

1. Michael and I highly recommend the best-selling book *American Icon*, by Bryce Hoffman, which chronicles Alan's experience in leading Ford's remarkable turnaround.

Chapter 17: Make a Difference in the World

1. Luke 12:47–49 Revised Geneva Translation, accessed June 19, 2022, https://www.biblegateway.com/passage/?search=Luke%2012%3A47-49&version=RGT, accessed June 19, 2022.

About the Authors

JOE HART began his career as a practicing attorney. After taking a Dale Carnegie Course, Joe reassessed his career path and future, ultimately leaving the practice of law, going to work for a top real estate company, and then founding an innovative e-learning company called InfoAlly. After selling that business five years later, Joe became the president of Asset Health, a US-based health and wellness company—all before becoming the president and CEO of Dale Carnegie in 2015. In 2019, the CEO Forum Group named Joe as one of twelve transformative leaders, giving him the Transformative CEO Leadership Award in the category of the People. He is the host of a top global podcast, *Take Command: A Dale Carnegie Podcast*, and he speaks around the world on topics such as leadership, resilience, and innovation, among other things. Joe and his wife, Katie, have six children, two dogs, and one cat. He is an active marathoner, having run many races, including Boston, New York, Chicago, Berlin, Detroit, and Toronto.

MICHAEL CROM retired from a thirty-five-year career at Dale Carnegie Training. He served most recently as chief learning officer and executive vice president. Michael continues to serve on Dale Carnegie's board of directors. He is an active member of his community, serving as a church elder, a Financial Peace University facilitator, and a teacher at his local Boys & Girls Club. Before *Take Command*, Michael coauthored *The Sales Advantage* and *The Leader in You: How to Win Friends, Influence People, and Succeed in a Changing World*. Michael and his wife, Nancy, have two wonderful adult children, Nicole and Alex.